Critical Guides to Spanish Texts

EDITED BY J. E. VAREY AND A. D. DEYERMOND

Critical Guides to Spanish Texts

TIRSO DE MOLINA

El burlador de Sevilla

Daniel Rogers

Senior Lecturer in Spanish, University of Durham

Grant & Cutler Ltd *in association with*
Tamesis Books Ltd 1977

© Grant and Cutler Ltd 1977

ISBN 0 7293 0039 0

Printed in England at
The Compton Press Ltd
Tisbury, Wilts.
for
GRANT & CUTLER LTD
11 BUCKINGHAM STREET, LONDON, W.C.2.

Contents

Prefatory Note

All references to *El burlador de Sevilla* are to the edition by Américo Castro, Clásicos Castellanos, 8th edition (Madrid, 1967). References to *Tan largo me lo fiáis* are to the edition by Xavier A. Fernández (Madrid, 1967). References to the Bibliographical Note are given by a number in italics, followed, where necessary, by a page-reference.

Five people in particular have helped me with this book. I would like to thank them all. Dr A. E. Sloman, Vice-Chancellor of the University of Essex, kindly allowed me to make use of his meticulous transcription of the two early versions of the play; Mr A. A. Heathcote of the University of Sheffield suggested some additions to the critical bibliography (though the selection and comments are my own); the Editors, Professors J. E. Varey and A. D. Deyermond, have been helpfully critical, encouraging and above all patient; finally, their task and mine has been made very much easier by the obliging efficiency of Mrs B. A. McDonald, Secretary to the Department of Spanish at Durham, who can produce a presentable typescript from anything put in front of her, "aunque sean los papeles rotos de las calles".

As a postscript to Chapter 1, I would add that Dr D. W. Cruickshank of University College Dublin has kindly allowed me to quote his opinion, based on typographical evidence, that *B* was printed by Manuel de Sande of Seville, ca. 1627–9.

Lanchester
1976

Introduction

"Un hombre sin nombre"

When the Duchess Isabela leads Don Juan through the door into the imaginary darkness of the sunlit *corral* stage, neither she nor the audience knows who he is. Isabela thinks he is the Duke Octavio:

> Duque Octavio, por aquí
> podrás salir más seguro. (I, 1–2)

An audience used to picking up information at the beginning of a play is bound to think so too – until his sudden threat to put out her light tells her and them that something is wrong. The Duchess's midnight visitor is not the Duke but "un hombre sin nombre". The audience soon hears that he is the nephew of the Spanish ambassador to Naples, Don Pedro Tenorio; but not until more than half-way through the first Act, when they see him carried ashore at Tarragona (I, 577–8), is Don Juan Tenorio named.

The figure of Don Juan Tenorio has since become world-famous. He is one of the very few heroes in modern literature (Faust is another) who have so outgrown the work in which they first appeared, and been taken over by so many different writers, that they may be thought of as having some kind of independent existence. Not even Hamlet or Don Quixote has passed into mythology in this way. In this respect Don Juan has become a legendary hero more like Ulysses or King Arthur. He has appeared in so many different plays, operas, poems and novels that it is difficult to imagine the reaction of an audience who had never heard of him. It is hard to see the first Don Juan for what he is, or the first Don Juan play for what it is, and not bring in what we have heard and felt about later ones – especially as we have only a rough idea of what the first Don Juan play must have been like.

All that is left of it are two garbled and conflicting versions, both of very dubious origin. We cannot be sure who wrote the first play with Don Juan in it, or when he wrote it, or exactly what he wrote.

The two surviving versions do at least agree on the outline of the story, on the names of nearly all the characters, and on enough of their lines for us to speak of two versions rather than two plays. These two versions are probably as close as we shall ever come to the original Don Juan play. Whether the lost original was a perfect work of art is something we may never know. What we do know is that one of the garbled versions, *El burlador de Sevilla*, had the vitality to excite the world's imagination.

The puzzle of the two versions

There must once have been an author's manuscript, which may or
may not have been copied before being sold to a company of actors.
The *autor de comedias*, or director of the company, would certainly have made alterations to the script before it was performed.
All that now survive are two early printed versions. One is entitled
El burlador de Sevilla y convidado de piedra and appears in a collection of *Doce comedias nuevas de Lope de Vega y otros autores*
published in Barcelona by Gerónimo Margarit and dated 1630.
The title-page describes it as a "comedia famosa del Maestro Tirso
de Molina" and says it was performed by Roque de Figueroa. The
other version is entitled *Tan largo me lo fiáis* (after Don Juan's
motto). It was published by itself, with no date or printer's name,
and described as a "comedia famosa de Don Pedro Calderón".

The credentials of these two versions have puzzled scholars ever
since the only known copy of *Tan largo* was discovered nearly a
hundred years ago (1878). Which version came first? How does it
come about that there are two versions so nearly the same and yet
so different?

So far, no one has been able to tell exactly when either of them
was first printed, let alone written. The leaf-numbers in the Barcelona 1630 book show that ten of the plays in it had been printed
separately (the leaves of each play are numbered from 1, except for
the last play where they are not numbered) and that the remaining
two, *De este agua no beberé* and *El burlador de Sevilla*, with leaves
numbered 41–60 and 61–82, must have belonged to a book of plays
printed before Margarit's collection. The dates on made-up vol-
umes like Margarit's were often false. In this case Margarit is trying to sell old plays as new. He would not want to pretend they
had been printed earlier than they had been. We are probably safe
in believing that the plays in his collection had been written, performed and printed before 1630.

The single surviving copy of *Tan largo* has been judged from the look of the paper and the type to date from about 1660.[1] This does not mean that the text of *Tan largo* was written as late as that, nor even that it was written later than the text of *El burlador*. In fact, if we compare the two texts we can see that *Tan largo* must often be more faithful to the original (*29, 30, 31*).

Before this very complicated state of affairs can be made at all clear some of the differences between the two versions need to be described. Measured by the number of lines, the greatest single difference is that in Act I of *El burlador* (which we shall call *B*) Don Gonzalo has a speech of 136 lines in praise of Lisbon (I, 722–858). This speech is not in *Tan largo* (which we shall call *TL*). Instead, Don Juan himself gives a 260-line description of Seville in Act II (*32*, II, 119–380). At first sight, neither of these long speeches has much to do with the rest of the play. Either of them could have been put in, and the other cut out, to suit a particular occasion. But at both points there are small clues to which version must have come first. In *TL* the whole scene between Don Gonzalo and the King is written in *octavas*. In *B* the exchanges between Don Gonzalo and the King are in blank verse, and Don Gonzalo's praise of Lisbon is in *romance*. A change from *octavas* to blank verse is more likely than one the other way (*31*). In addition, *TL*'s anachronistic reference to Goa (probably introduced to rhyme with "Lisboa") seems to have been modified in *B* (I, 701–4). In Act II, Octavio's remark to Don Juan that all praise of Seville must fall short (*B*, II, 130–7), which occurs in both versions, makes better sense if Don Juan has just been praising the city. It looks, then, as if *TL*'s Seville speech was cut out and *B*'s Lisbon speech put in. That is, as if *TL* must have come first.

The second major difference is that towards the end of *B* there are two short scenes involving Aminta which are not in *TL* (*B*, III, 788–836; 1007–13), whereas *TL* has a short scene between Don Juan's father and Mota which is not in *B*. These scenes affect the action more than do the speeches of city-praise, but it is harder to see which are later additions, and which come from the original.

To make matters even more complicated, there are a number of important scenes where either version could be a paraphrase of the other: the same amount of action is gone through, much the same

---

[1] *Comedias de Tirso de Molina*, ed. E. Cotarelo, II (Madrid, 1907), p. vii.

information is put across, roughly the same attitudes and feelings are expressed, yet the wording is almost completely different.

More bewildering still, even within these scenes, the first few lines and the last few are sometimes identical; and even in the middle of a speech the two versions will suddenly come together for a line or two and then part company. In other scenes the same stanzas appear in each version, but in a different order. Even in scenes which are nearly identical there will be four or five additional lines in one version or the other, and there are hundreds of lines where only a word or two are different.

There are also some differences in characters' names. In *TL* Don Juan's father is "Don Juan Tenorio el viejo"; in *B* he is Don Diego. In *TL* two of the girls are called Trisbea and Arminta, instead of Tisbea and Aminta. In *TL* it is Don Pedro Tenorio who goes with Isabela to Seville; in *B* it is a servant called Fabio. None of these changes matters much, but in the case of Don Juan's father it is fairly clear that he must originally have been called Don Juan: there are lines in both versions which would have no point unless father and son had the same name (*B*, II, 669–70). In this detail at least, *TL* must be closer to the original.[2]

There are many other points where the verse-forms or the wording show that *TL*'s must be the earlier reading. It is also obvious that *B*'s text is much the more corrupt. *B* has dozens of lines which do not rhyme, or do not scan, as they should; others make no sense, or less sense than the corresponding lines of *TL*. *TL* on the other hand is probably a cut version of the original. Acts I and III are both shorter than the usual 1000 lines or so; at one point in Act III there is mention of an arrangement for Don Juan's wedding which has not been referred to before, but which is discussed in *B*. There is no need to suppose that all the extra lines in *B* were added later. Nor is *TL*'s reading always preferable: in at least three places *B*'s versification is correct where *TL* has gone wrong (*31*). We can only guess at what was in the original play; but even to do this we need to use both the versions that are left.

These oddities cannot be the result of straightforward 'textual transmission' (text A being gradually transformed into text X

<hr/>

[2] Credit for this discovery must go to Blanca de los Ríos (Tirso de Molina, *Obras dramáticas completas*, II [Madrid, 1952], pp. 553b–554a, 664b).

through an accumulation of conscious and unconscious alterations
as text B is copied from text A, C from B and so forth) : no one with
one of these versions in front of him could have written the other.
But what about someone trying to reconstruct the original without
a text to copy from, that is, from memory? Such a person might
well remember the beginnings and ends of scenes. He might, if he
were practised at it, remember roughly what happened in each
scene. Even where he remembered whole passages by heart he
would get a word wrong here and there; even where he had forgotten almost the whole passage a few lines might come back to
him. This theory of reconstruction from memory may account for
most of the differences between *El burlador* and *Tan largo*. Since
both are printed texts, there is the usual crop of printers' errors
and interferences as well.

As we have seen, *TL,* where it is not cut, is probably closer to
the original. With its cuts, its correct versification and scanty stage-
directions, *TL* probably derives from the original through a written tradition. Probably through successive printings it has been cut
and tidied for the reading public, and then attributed to a famous
living playwright in the hope of increasing the sales. *B* with its
insertions and inaccuracies and its detailed stage-directions is probably the version reconstructed from memory by theatre people.

Three different sorts of people might have been trying to piece
together a play from memory : the playwright himself (if he had
sold his manuscript to a company and later wanted to publish the
play in book form); a company of actors wanting to revive the play
after their copies (or their company) had disintegrated; a *memo-
rión,* or professional memory-man employed by another company
to attend their performances and pirate their plays (*30*). The first
of these possibilities is the most attractive, but probably the most
remote : even if he had kept a synopsis[3] it is unlikely that the playwright could have remembered word for word so much of what he
had written. Either of the other possibilities is much more likely.
Perhaps the truth lies somewhere between them. As it happens,
Roque de Figueroa had in his company an actor called Pedro de

[3] Cf. Lope de Vega, *Arte nuevo de hacer comedias en este tiempo,* in *Comedias,*
ed. Luis Guarner, II (Barcelona, 1955), p. 400: "El sujeto elegido escriba en
prosa". Was this how he and his followers worked?

Pernia who was reputed to be capable of rewriting plays in emergencies:

> Que hace versos, que remedia,
> si sucede una desgracia
> doce o diez y seis colunas
> de la noche a la mañana.[4]

The original Don Juan play obviously suffered several misfortunes. Roque de Figueroa's company is said to have performed a version of *B*. Pedro de Pernia looks a likely man to have done the repairs. However the company came by their reconstructed script, the *autor de comedias* would then have altered it further for performance by his troupe. (For instance, Isabela's escort to Seville would have had to become "Fabio" if the parts of Don Diego Tenorio and his brother Don Pedro were being doubled.) Then as now, it is quite likely that actors and actor-managers had as good an understanding of the stage as any playwright. If bits of *B* are better theatre than the corresponding bits of *TL* – and the opening scene certainly is – this may simply be because they have been touched up by people with a working knowledge of the theatre.

Authorship

If anything is clear amid all this uncertainty it is that we do not know who wrote the original play. No one, as far as I know, has tried to argue that Calderón wrote *TL* (*32*, xxiv). A case has been put forward for Andrés de Claramonte as the *refundidor* responsible for *B* (*34*). Claramonte's name is on *De este agua no beberé*, the play which appeared next to *B* in the volume rehashed by Margarit. Four lines of the two plays (*B*, III, 1–4) are almost identical. Two character names (Don Diego Tenorio and Tisbea) occur in both. Claramonte was a notorious plagiarist as well as an *autor de comedias*. He may at some time have had something to do with a performance or a printing of *B*. On such slender evidence there is no need to conclude that he wrote it.

---

[4] Quiñones de Benavente, quoted by H. A. Rennert, *The Spanish Stage in the Time of Lope de Vega* (New York, 1909; repr. 1963), p. 172 n. Pernia was with Roque's company in 1628 and had previously (1623) been with Balbín's. See Hannah E. Bergman, *Luis Quiñones de Benavente y sus entremeses* (Madrid, 1965), p. 523.

That Tirso de Molina wrote the original from which *TL* and *B*
derive has generally been taken for granted. The best evidence that
he did is the appearance of his name on the title-page of *B*. In the
present state of our knowledge (and the attribution of doubtful
comedias is still largely guess-work) there is no particular reason
either to believe or disbelieve this attribution. The versification, im-
perfect as it is, is within the range of Tirso's normal practice.[5] The
probable date of composition (see below) falls within the span of
Tirso's writing life. Resemblances to plays known to be by Tirso
have been exaggerated, but at least there is nothing in *B* which is
glaringly inconsistent with the work of this highly inconsistent
dramatist. *B* does not appear in any of the *Partes* in which the plays
of Tirso were collected; but then the five *Partes*, with twelve plays
in each (and not all of these plays authentic!), contain only a small
fraction of his output (by 1621 he claimed to have written three
hundred plays). What little we know does not rule out the attribution to Tirso, but the most that can be said in support of it is that
it is early (earlier than Margarit), that it has been long and widely
repeated and that it has never been seriously challenged.

Date (1616–1625)

We have seen that the dates of *TL* and *B* are uncertain. The date
of the lost original is anybody's guess. Tirso de Molina may have
written it in 1616 while in Seville on his way to the Indies (*34*). But,
supposing he wrote it at all, he could just as well have done so
before going to Seville, or after he came back from Santo Domingo
in 1618. The Lisbon speech in *B* may have something to do with
Philip III's visit there in 1619. *B*'s closing lines may refer to a
scandal current in 1617 (*34*). In that year the church and convent
of St Francis in Madrid were being renovated. The monument to
Henry IV's queen, Juana de Portugal, was romoved and there
was a rumour that a prominent nobleman planned to replace it
with a memorial to his own family. The removal of the queen's
remains and the attempt to discredit her caused some indignation

---

[5] See S. Griswold Morley, "The Use of Verse-Forms (Strophes) by Tirso de
Molina", *Bulletin Hispanique*, VII (1905), 387-408, and "El uso de las combina-
ciones métricas de las comedias de Tirso de Molina", *Bulletin Hispanique*, XVI
(1914), 177-208.

in the capital. The idea of bringing the Commander's memorial to the same church (instead of to St John's in Toro, the church mentioned in *TL*, and the traditional burial place of the historical Ulloas) might have raised a cheap laugh in Madrid in 1617. The rest of *B* could still have been written before that year : a topical reference could easily have been tacked on to the end of an old play. Roque de Figueroa is not recorded as having his own company until 1624 (in the previous year he was with Domingo Balbín).[6] There is mention of a performance in Naples of a play called *Il convitato di pietra* in 1625.[7] This was done by Pedro Osorio's company, presumably in Spanish. Osorio, like Roque de Figueroa, had been in Balbín's company (in 1609 and 1613) before setting up his own.[8] Perhaps the original Don Juan play was in Balbín's repertoire. At any rate the original must have been in existence by 1625. Topical references in *B* may go back, as we have seen, to 1619 or even 1617, which takes the original back almost to the year of Tirso's stay in Seville (1616). Unless we are to suppose that the version performed by Osorio goes back to his days with Balbín (and we cannot be sure these came to an end in 1613), there is no reason to believe that the original play dates from before 1616.

Sources

Don Juan's stone guest comes from folklore. The Burlador himself seems to have come out of the dramatist's head. Stories about an exchange of invitations between a live man and a dead one have been traced all over Europe and as far away as Iceland.[9] Spanish folktales and ballads telling such stories survived in oral tradition at least until the early years of this century.[10] According to these

---

[6] See E. Cotarelo y Mori, *Tirso de Molina: investigaciones biobibliográficas* (Madrid, 1893), pp. 203-6; C. Pérez Pastor, *Nuevos datos acerca del histrionismo español en los siglos XVI y XVII*, Primera Serie (Madrid, 1901), Segunda Serie (Bordeaux, 1914); H. A. Rennert, *The Spanish Stage in the Time of Lope de Vega* (New York, 1909; repr. 1963).

[7] See Joseph G. Fucilla, *"El convidado de piedra* in Naples in 1625", *Bulletin of the Comediantes*, X, 1 (1958), 5-6.

[8] Cotarelo (see note 6, above).

[9] See Dorothy McKay, *The Double Invitation in the Legend of Don Juan* (Stanford and London, 1943).

[10] R. Menéndez Pidal, "Sobre los orígenes de *El convidado de piedra*", in *Estudios literarios*, 6th ed. (Buenos Aires, Colección Austral, 1946), pp. 89-113.

tales a young man invites a dead "man", generally a skeleton or a skull, to supper. The dead "man" turns up and returns the invitation. The story has various endings. Sometimes with the help of holy water or relics the young man escapes with his life but learns to show more respect for the dead; sometimes he dies of fright; in one Spanish version, he becomes a priest. Dorothy McKay's wide survey of the double invitation legend draws the interesting conclusion that the statue, as distinct from a skeleton or skull, is peculiar to versions found in the Iberian Peninsula. A folktale or a ballad, then, probably provides the basis of *El burlador de Sevilla*'s supernatural ending.

Attempts to find a source for Don Juan Tenorio have been less successful and less illuminating. Dissolute young aristocrats of roughly similar type were common in the seventeenth century, both on the stage and in real life, but the idea of the "burlador", the young man who made a speciality of the deception of women, seems first to have crystallized in the original of our play. In a few of the ballads the young man is reported to be going to Mass to look at the women rather than to worship God, but this hardly makes him a Don Juan.

What appears to have happened is that the inventor of the *Burlador* took over a traditional story of the supernatural as an ending for his play; or that in expanding the traditional story he invented a young man for whom this story would provide a fitting end. The order of events will probably never be known and does not matter. What do matter are the links which the playwright forged between the ready-made ending and the rest of his play. In an essay written more than ten years ago I tried to describe these links (*10*). I now think I exaggerated the importance and subtlety of some of them, but I still believe that the playwright adopted and adapted the double invitation legend in order to dramatize the idea of retribution.

Don Juan's motto "tan largo me lo fiáis" has also been traced to a popular tradition. In a collection of folktales made by the Valencian bookseller, poet and actor Juan de Timoneda (d. 1583), *El buen aviso y portacuentos* (Valencia, 1564), Libro I, cuento v, there is a story of a student set upon by *capeadores* (cloak-thieves). He tells them that in the next world they will pay for what they have done. One of the thieves replies:

> viendo hermano que burláis
> de los dos, y de tal modo
> con el lienzo amenazáis,
> menester lo habemos todo,
> pues *tan largo lo fiáis*.[11]

The use of this phrase in reply to a threat of future punishment in the next world strongly suggests that the playwright knew this story or one like it.

Like many *comedias* by Lope and his followers, this one draws on popular traditions. As also often happens, the sources do not completely account for the play.

[11] See W. L. Fichter and F. Sánchez Escribano, "Una anécdota folklórica del *Tan largo me lo fiáis* no notada hasta la fecha", *Revista de Filología Hispánica*, IV (1942), 70-2.

2 Staging

To try to imagine how the play may have worked we need to know roughly what sort of theatre it was written for. The *corrales* had a deep, almost square, stage jutting well out into the auditorium. Characters came on and went off through two doorways at the back of the stage. Above these was a gallery supported on pillars. This gallery could be used for balcony-scenes or to represent the walls of a city, the deck of a ship or even the side of a mountain. At either end of it there were steps leading down to the stage. Below the gallery and between the stage-doors was a curtained 'discovery space' or inner stage. There was no front curtain (part of the audience watched from the sides); no artificial lighting (performances were in the afternoon) and no scenery except for a few simple props. Costumes were modern (i.e. seventeenth-century). Altogether, performances must have been quite like the ones in Elizabethan England, except that in Spain the female parts were not played by boys.[1]

As in the Elizabethan theatre (or in any other) the layout of the stage and the auditorium and the equipment available made a difference to what the dramatists wrote. Writing for a stage with no scenery or lighting, for instance, a playwright had to remember fairly early on in each scene to let the audience know where the action was supposed to be taking place (if this mattered) and what time of day or night it was. Even lyrical descriptions like the one in Tisbea's first speech (I, 375–481) arise out of this basic need. Characters in Shaw or Chekhov do not describe the drawing-room furniture (though the stage-directions may) because the audience can see it. In the opening scene of *El burlador*, Isabela's "Quiero sacar una luz" tells the audience it is dark, although they have probably guessed as much from the way she and Don Juan creep in and talk in whispers (and perhaps she is wearing a nightgown). Ripio begins his scene with Octavio by telling us it is morning (I, 191). Tisbea begins her soliloquy by describing the seashore (I, 375–481).

[1] For a full account see N. D. Shergold, *A History of the Spanish Stage from Medieval Times until the End of the Seventeenth Century* (Oxford, 1967).

When Octavio meets Don Juan in Act II they both must know where they are: it is the audience who need to be told they are now in Seville (II, 121). The rustic song "Lindo sale el sol de abril" (II, 633) announces that we are out in the country again, on an April morning. Act III begins towards nightfall. Batricio grumbles about Don Juan's behaviour at supper. During his soliloquy, Don Juan glances at the stars. Aminta is getting ready for bed. Isabela and Fabio are by the sea at Tarragona (III, 313–18). In the previous scene the inner stage was probably brought into use as Aminta's bedroom. A more spectacular use of it is the discovery of Don Gonzalo's tomb. In the next scene two servants bring on a table and lay it for Don Juan's supper: clearly they are in the "posada" mentioned in the previous scene (III, 474). After the exit of the statue and Don Juan's soliloquy the entry of the King and Don Diego takes us back to the palace (III, 688). The next scene with Don Juan and Catalinón shows how on the *corral* stage the location could sometimes shift without interrupting the action (more commonly the stage was cleared and a new set of characters came on). As they talk, Don Juan and Catalinón arrive outside the church ("Ya está cerrada la iglesia", III, 873). Don Juan insists that they knock on the door and go in. After the stage direction "Entran por una puerta y salen por otra" they are inside the church: "¡Qué escura que está la iglesia!" (III, 883). All they have had to do is go off through one of the doors at the back of the stage and come on through the other. After the spectacular climax the final scenes take place at the palace. There being no front curtain, the end of the play is announced in the closing lines.

There is only one *tramoya*, or special mechanical effect, called for in this play: the collapse of the tomb and the disappearance of Don Juan and Don Gonzalo through the floor "con mucho ruido" (III, 974). This would have needed a trapdoor (which the *corrales* had)[2] and probably a few thunderflashes. The other sensational feature of the staging is, of course, the "convidado de piedra", the moving statue. As at the climax, the directions in *B* are much more explicit than those in *TL*. Whoever wrote them was giving instructions for a calculated *coup de théâtre*. Nevertheless, they do not tell

---

[2] Shergold, p. 208. *TL*'s stage direction provides for an alternative: "Tiran el carretón, o se hunden Don Juan y Don Gonzalo" (*32*, p. 77).

us exactly how the statue was to be represented. At its "discovery", the effigy is probably lying on its back on the tomb (cf. Don Juan's taunt, "importa no estar dormido", III, 468). This would add considerably to the shock of seeing him upright when he comes on after the ominous knocking. The memorial ordered by the King was to be made of bronze and "piedras varias". The statue itself is always described as being made of stone. The simplest if not the most spectacular means of presenting the statue would have been for the actor playing Don Gonzalo to pose as the recumbent effigy (polychrome statuary was common at this period) and later come on, more or less unchanged, as the statue come to life. Alternatively the actor could have posed in a grey cloak and gloves and with his face painted or masked. More likely he was completely encased in armour, as *TL*'s stage-direction (32, 69) indicates. It is even possible that some kind of automaton was used.[3] Such things were within the range of seventeenth-century technology, though not every company of actors could have afforded one. At his first "walk-on" appearance the stage direction is very specific about movements and refers to the statue's "pasos menudos" (III, 533). One supposes that he is not to scuttle but to inch his way forward with the slow menace of a robot. He later nods his head, makes signs with his hands and, when at last he and Don Juan are alone together, the actor is told to speak "paso, como cosa del otro mundo". This is not very helpful but seems to call for some kind of hollow whisper. If so, it would have had to be a good "stage whisper": his words are so important that they must be heard all over the house.

"Lo alto", as the gallery was called, does not seem to be needed for this play at all. It is perhaps surprising that the great philanderer is not given a balcony-scene. The woman who hands Ana's letter through the *reja* could do so either from the gallery or through the curtains of the inner stage. Don Juan's remark about "la estafeta del viento" (II, 265) may mean that the letter came fluttering down to him from above. He does not, like other *galanes*, look up to his *damas*, serenading them from below, but meets them on his own level.

[3] On the origins of automata and on their use in medieval and Golden-Age Spain see J. E. Varey, *Historia de los títeres en España (desde sus orígenes hasta mediados del siglo XVIII)* (Madrid, 1957), pp. 24-90.

Three other aspects of staging deserve to be mentioned: asides, soliloquies and songs. Asides and soliloquies are two stage conventions which probably work better in a theatre where actors are close to the audience and not cut off by a proscenium, footlights or an orchestra pit. Don Juan hardly has time for soliloquies, though there are a few in the play, but asides in which he takes the audience into his confidence, involving them in his *burlas*, are a vital part of his role. As well as performing for their benefit, Don Juan speaks to his audience direct. Before all else his is a part to be played in a *corral*.

Golden-Age plays regularly had songs in them and theatre companies normally included musicians and singers. The songs were often used for choric comment on the action. In this play the use of song is tellingly ironic.

In Act I the song of the fishermen comes immediately before the entrance of the distracted Tisbea:

> A pescar salió la niña
> tendiendo redes;
> y, en lugar de peces,
> las almas prende. (I, 981-4)

With its facile sub-petrarchan conceit about netting hearts,[4] this song presents the fishergirl as earlier she saw herself. In the meantime the audience have watched her change. They know well enough what is now happening off-stage. Then, as the melodious voices trail away, on comes Tisbea, changed more drastically still: dishevelled, demented and screaming for revenge.

The first snatch of song in Act II (456-7) is also in ironic contrast to what the audience knows is going on – a trite serenade about a lover's impatience just when Don Juan has seen his opportunity to trick the Marquis and Ana. When the same snatch is sung again (511-12) the last note, like that of the fisherman's song,

[4] In Petrarch (e.g. *Rime* CLXXX, 1-2, LIX, 4-5 [Francesco Petrarca, *Rime e Trionfi*, ed Ferdinando Neri, 2nd ed., Turin 1960, pp. 277, 115]) and his Spanish imitators (e.g. Garcilaso, *Canción* IV, 101-2, in *Poesías castellanas completas*, ed. Elias L. Rivers, Clásicos Castalia, Madrid, 1969, p. 90) the net in which the lover (or his soul or reason) was caught was commonly woven from the girl's golden hair. Don Juan expresses a similar idea at I, 938-9. The application of this metaphor to a fishergirl with a real net is similar to Don Juan's application of other petrarchan metaphors of storm and shipwreck (see p. 56 below).   .

is immediately followed by a woman's screams. Reading the printed page, one can easily miss the effectiveness of this; the effect can only be appreciated, as it could only be devised, by imagining how it would sound.

The next song, at the beginning of the country wedding scene (II, 633), marks an abrupt change of scene and mood. The King has just spoken an epitaph on the murdered Commander. The stage is cleared and on come the singers, now dressed as shepherds, singing of clover and lemon-balm and the beauty of a bride on a sunny April morning. Into this harmonious idyll comes Catalinón announcing the arrival of Don Juan on his way to Lebrija. At the end of the Act, with the bridegroom muttering his forebodings and Catalinón predicting the fate of his master's fourth victim, the singers strike up once more. Their song may be the same[5]: "Lindo sale el sol de abril"; but the day has clouded over.

In Act III when the statue comes to supper with Don Juan the singers perform as an accompaniment to the meal (582–5, 594–601). Once again a trite song of love is used ironically in an incongruous situation. Finally in the second supper-scene the same refrain ("¡qué largo me lo fiáis!") is taken up and explicitly condemned:

> Mientras en el mundo viva,
> no es justo que diga nadie:
> "¡qué largo me lo fiáis!"
> siendo tan breve el cobrarse. (III, 938–41)

In context, this is a final warning to Don Juan.

At the same time it provides an easily recognizable link with the first supper-scene (especially if sung to the same tune). It can also be taken as a general warning to all mortals. These last four lines of song embody the moral message of the whole play.

[5] *B*'s text does not tell the *músicos* what to sing, but in *TL* the Act ends with the first two lines of the song as before.

3 Plot

By the time *El burlador de Sevilla* was written, Lope de Vega had
worked out in practice and set out in theory a formula for holding
the attention of the most restless Spanish audience:

> En el acto primero ponga el caso.
> En el segundo enlace los sucesos
> de suerte que hasta medio del tercero
> apenas juzgue nadie en lo que para.[1]

Most *comedias*, from the most frivolous to the most profound, fol-
low this plan: some strange case is abruptly presented; unforeseen
complications arise and the outcome is not decided until the last
minute. Of course the same is true of a lot of non-Spanish plays
and films, particularly thrillers and light entertainments, but this
is not the only way a play can work: consider for instance *Oedipus
Rex, Phèdre, Waiting for Godot, Look Back in Anger. El burlador*
presents an important variation on Lope's formula: the complications come before the "caso" is made clear. The Burlador is not
first shown preparing to play a trick on a lady – he has just done it.
In fact the playwright begins by playing a trick on his audience:
the 'Duke Octavio' is not the Duke Octavio at all (the kind of
revelation that is more usual in the last scenes of plays than in the
first). The audience are as bewildered as Isabela. From then on,
while the other characters try to sort out the confusion and patch
up the damage, Don Juan is always ahead of them. This gives the
play the pace and excitement of a chase. Before the Isabela scandal
has been glossed over, Don Juan has already marked out Tisbea as
his next victim. As he waits for nightfall, the audience are shown
Alfonso XI of Castile, still unaware of the Naples affair, arranging
for him to marry Doña Ana de Ulloa. By the time the king hears
about the Naples escapade and decrees that Don Juan shall marry
Isabela, Tisbea has been abandoned and Don Juan is preparing to
trick Doña Ana. The king has just had Mota arrested for the

---

[1] *Arte nuevo de hacer comedias* (see Chap. 1, n. 3), p. 402.

murder of Don Gonzalo when Don Juan arrives at Aminta's wedding. As soon as Don Juan goes off with Aminta, all his other victims are seen heading for the palace to demand their due. Don Juan's last adventure keeps him, as always, one step ahead of his pursuers. Before he can appear for his betrothral to Isabela he has another appointment. By the time all the victims are gathered round the king and the king sentences Don Juan to death, the Burlador is already dead.

After the first "burla", when they are themselves deceived, the audience know more than the victims. Through his asides the audience know that Don Juan is not really sorry for deceiving Isabela; they know that he is going back to Spain, even though he has promised his uncle he will go to Sicily or Milan. Through his words to Catalinón, they know better than to believe his lyrical protestations to Tisbea. They know that when he puts on Mota's cloak he is going to visit not Beatriz, but Mota's Ana. They know he does not mean to marry Aminta and that he is lying to Batricio. Made a party to each of Don Juan's "burlas", the audience are invited to share Don Juan's amusement at his scandalous attacks on things they have been brought up to respect (6, 15).

At the same time their sense of justice and propriety will tell them that things can't go on like this: they are witnessing a series of wrongs which are crying out to be put right. This is what provides the play's suspense: as the mouse's games grow more and more outrageous, the audience are waiting for the cat.

Don Juan takes the audience into his confidence. Don Gonzalo does not. The statue gives no sign that it will accept Don Juan's impudent invitation. When the knock comes on the door the audience do not know (though, like Don Juan, they may guess) who is there. When the statue holds out its hand and tells Don Juan not to be afraid, they do not know how much the statue's grip is going to hurt. They do not know any more than Don Juan does what will happen at the second supper. The service, the menu and the singing all make plain that Don Juan is to be taught a severe lesson; but again as the statue holds out its hand to him, it tells him not to be afraid. Only when he takes the statue's hand the second time does Don Juan cry out. He is being burnt. The audience were not prepared any more than the victim for this piece of deception.

But the "burla" is not yet complete. Don Juan puts up a fight, tries to argue that he is not guilty, and, at last, asks for a confessor. (Here, as in the opening scene, the text of *El burlador* is dramatically far better than *Tan largo*'s, where he asks for a confessor before resorting to force.) The rake is ready to repent. Surely this is the moment that all the warnings of death, judgement and hell (not to mention Don Juan's catchphrase) have been leading up to? Will there be Angels' voices? A kindly old hermit? A touching reconciliation with Don Diego?

> No hay lugar; ya acuerdas tarde . . .
> Esta es justicia de Dios :
> quien tal hace que tal pague. (III, 968–71)

Now that Don Juan's story is so well-known it may be difficult to remember that his headlong progress begins and ends with a dramatic surprise,

> de suerte que . . .
> apenas juzgue nadie en lo que para.

First the audience is deceived by Don Juan. Then they watch him deceiving others. Finally they see him deceived. But this time the audience have not been primed beforehand. Don Juan and his audience are shown the truth together. Together they are made to stare damnation in the face.

4 *Characterization*

In seventeenth-century Spanish drama character is less important than action (27). The story is the main thing, and the point of the story is the point of the play. But in this *comedia* more than in many others the action arises from the character of the hero. The situations devised by the playwright for the entertainment of his audience are presented as being devised by the main character for his own amusement. They take the form they do because of the special kind of person he is.

Don Juan

So much has been written about Don Juan as though he were a real person that we had better begin by considering him as a stage role – a part for an actor to play. So considered, he is superb: essentially theatrical;[1] perfectly suited to the kind of stage and the kind of audience for which he was created. Not that he has any great poetry to speak, nor many big speeches (his longest in *B* is a soliloquy of just over forty short lines). Except when he is wooing a girl or talking his way out of trouble, he is a man of few words: sharp commands, brusque rejoinders, jeering asides. A few of these are memorable, but three other things go further towards explaining his theatrical appeal: his impatient desire for action, his love of creating dramatic situations, and his vital and changing relationship to his audience.

Don Juan is always in a hurry. He is quick to accept his uncle's offer of escape (I, 106–11). "Esta noche he de gozalla" he says of Tisbea just after their first brief meeting (I, 686). Even before he has achieved his aim he is arranging his escape ("Esas dos yeguas prevén", I, 877). Reproached by his father in the middle of his arrangements to deceive the Marquis, he turns abruptly back to his plans as soon as the old man has gone (II, 427–30). Threatened

---

[1] "El carácter de Don Juan Tenorio es el más teatral que se ha visto sobre las tablas desde que hay representaciones" (Esteban de Arteaga, *Investigaciones filosóficas sobre la belleza ideal* [Madrid, 1789], p. 73, quoted in *3*).

by Don Gonzalo, he wastes no time in arguing ("¡Muere, traidor!
– Desta suerte/muero", II, 533–4). Arriving by chance at Aminta's
wedding, he sits down beside the bride as soon as he sees her (II,
714–15). Later he in the same breath assures her father that he will
marry her and orders his servant to saddle the horses for the ride
back to Seville ("Mi esposa decid. Ensilla,/Catalinón." III, 152–3).
A little later he allows himself one brief soliloquy :

> La noche en negro silencio
> se estiende, y ya las cabrillas
> entre racimos de estrellas
> el polo más alto pisan. (III, 193–6)

Then he turns at once from lyricism to the job in hand :

> Yo quiero poner mi engaño
> por obra. (III, 197–8)

A moment of grandiose reflection –

> El amor me guía
> a mi inclinación, de quien
> no hay hombre que se resista (III, 198–200)

– in which his lust is suddenly promoted to the status of an irresist-
ible destiny – and then bed :

> Quiero llegar a la cama.
> ¡Aminta! (III, 201–2)

As soon as he reads the inscription on Don Gonzalo's tomb he
invites the Commander to supper that same night (III, 458–9). All
through the first supper scene he is testy and abrupt. Given a chance
to reflect after the statue has let go of his hand, he quickly dismisses his fears as imaginary and looks forward to the notoriety he
will win on the following night (III, 684–7). At his final meeting
with the statue he is still brusque and anxious to get on with things
("Di presto lo que me quieres . . . Cenemos . . . Ya he cenado; haz
que levanten la mesa" III, 897–946). With scarcely a hesitation he
gives the statue his hand.

In his *Arte nuevo* Lope de Vega refers to the restless impatience
of his audience :

> la cólera
> de un español sentado no se templa
> si no le representan en dos horas
> hasta el final juicio desde el Génesis.[2]

This tireless man of action must have been a hero after their own heart.

Don Juan is also a ready improviser of entertaining plots – of instant *comedias de capa y espada* – "in real life". Until the stone guest arrives for supper Don Juan makes up most of his own play : he sets the pace and devises the situations. Even his decision to keep his promise to the statue is taken for effect – "por que se admire y espante/Sevilla de mi valor" (III, 686–7), although as it turns out the spectacular finale is the work of another hand. As this "action playwright" improvises his play his relationship to his audience changes.

He begins by disconcerting them. Coming on as Duke Octavio, he suddenly turns out to be "un hombre sin nombre". To begin with, then, the audience are not simply told or shown that he is a "burlador"; they are made to feel "burlados". When the nameless intruder confronts the ambassador, the audience are as anxious as Don Pedro to know who he is and what he has done. But, as the story emerges, they learn more than Don Pedro does. After the nephew has knelt down and surrendered his sword, the uncle does not hear the aside (I, 115) about what the uncle has called "this sorry business" ("Para mí alegre, dirás"). Then, having promised faithfully to go into hiding in Sicily or Milan, the young man cheerfully tells the audience that he is off to Spain. Fellow-victims of his first "burla", the audience have now become his accomplices. The playwright has created a living character by bringing the audience to life.

By the time they see the passionate lyricist in action with Tisbea they already know he is not to be trusted. In case they have forgotten, Tisbea's own refrain "Plega a Dios que no mintáis" is enough to remind them. Before Don Juan and Tisbea are seen together again, Don Juan is shown arranging his means of escape, and he makes his intentions towards her quite explicit. As Tisbea comes on, the audience know what is in store for her. When Don Juan

[2] *Arte nuevo* (see Chap. I, n. 3), p. 400.

comes out with his romantic claptrap about King Love knowing no distinction between silk and sackcloth, the audience know very well that what they are watching is a performance.

From now until the discovery of Don Gonzalo's tomb near the middle of Act III, the audience are privileged to watch Don Juan deceiving other people. Thanks to his asides and to what they have already seen, they know more than the other characters on the stage. His words to Catalinón and Catalinón's aside ("cuando le vende le adula", II, 111) make them a party to his mock-apologies to the Duke he has dishonoured. They see his trick on the Marquis from the very beginning. They see his growing interest as Mota enthuses over his new love ("¿Tan bella es esa mujer?" II, 227). They see Ana's letter float as if by magic into his hands. They watch him revelling in his role ("Sevilla a voces me llama/el Bur-lador . . .", II, 269–70), rubbing his hands over the prospect of a fresh "burla" ("Gana me da de reír . . . Ya de la burla me río", II, 277–301); changing the time of the assignation from eleven o'clock to midnight. Better still, they see the benighted Marquis imagining that he himself is playing a trick on someone else. In Act III they are made a party to the deception of Aminta ("Mi esposa decid. Ensilla,/Catalinón." III, 152–3). This is going to be the best "burla" of all ("La burla más escogida/de todas ha de ser ésta", III, 160–1). In case anyone in the audience is fool enough to believe in the dazzling future he offers Aminta, there is his gloating aside as he goes off with her:

> ¡Qué mal conoces
> al Burlador de Sevilla! (III, 299–300)

One thing stands in the way of the audience's enjoyment of these tricks. The deception of Doña Ana went badly wrong. The Bur-lador was revealed as a ruthless killer, and as one who was prepared to let his friend be arrested for the murder. The moral susceptibili-ties of different members of an audience will vary. But by the time Don Juan invokes the dead in his pledge to Aminta (III, 277–82), they must all be feeling uneasy about the jokes they are being in-vited to share.

After Don Juan has read out Don Gonzalo's epitaph he may appear to retain the initiative, but in fact this is the moment when he loses it. His taunts, culminating in the invitation to supper, are a response to the challenge he sees in the inscription. Even before he came upon the tomb Don Juan was edgy and irritable, though he was still able to laugh at the idea of Aminta imagining herself as a lady (III, 437–41). From now on he hardly laughs again. During most of the first supper scene he does not mock but barks commands. Through his anger an uneasy audience can sense his unease. There is mockery implied in the words of the song he orders for his guest, and he is still able to laugh at the "burlas" of which these words remind him (III, 604). He can speak lightly of the statue's invitation even after the statue has taken his hand:

> Empresa mayor
> entendí que me pedías. (III, 651–2)

But his soliloquy immediately afterwards makes it obvious that he has been badly shaken. He dismisses his fears as imaginary. His exit-lines are exultant:

> Mañana iré a la capilla
> donde convidado soy,
> por que se admire y espante
> Sevilla de mi valor. (III, 684–7)

But this time the *sevillanos* and the audience are invited to marvel at his daring, not to share another joke.

In the second supper scene Don Juan may be pretending not to be afraid; but if so his pretence is entirely serious (it is also fatal). He is no longer playing the Burlador. A more serious role has been thrust upon him. Neither he nor his audience knows exactly what will happen. The final *tramoya* takes them both by surprise.

To sum up the shifting relationship between Don Juan and his audience, he begins by deceiving them; then he takes them into his confidence, and allows them to watch him deceiving others; finally the audience watch him being deceived by something which neither of them fully understands. Having been skilfully drawn into Don Juan's adventures, they can detach themselves only by disowning their hero (*15*).

Through the conventional medium of verse drama Don Juan is a portrayal of a recognizable human type. Having examined the workings of the theatrical role, we are now in a position to consider its human content. The character is not an ordinary "galán de comedia". Nor is he simply a lecherous and overbearing aristocrat like Lope's "comendadores". That he is lecherous and promiscuous goes without saying, but this does not distinguish him from, say, the Commander in *Fuenteovejuna*, the Duke in *El castigo sin venganza* or the Captain in *El alcalde de Zalamea*. In a way he is a "comendador" pretending to be a "galán", a lecher disguised as a lover. But the truly distinctive thing about him is that he adopts the pretence for fun – not just for the fulfilment of his physical desires, but for the malicious pleasure of deceit. Four main qualities seem to characterize his behaviour: deceitfulness, flippancy, malice and presumption. Deceiving and dishonouring are as important to him as sensual pleasure:

> el mayor
> gusto que en mí puede haber
> es burlar una mujer
> y dejalla sin honor. (II, 270–3)

His sexual desires are prompt and pressing ("Muerto voy/por la hermosa pescadora./Esta noche he de gozalla", I, 684–6). He is excited by Tisbea's hair and eyes and by Aminta's hands. But he has never seen Ana before he tries to deceive her: his interest is aroused merely by Mota's enthusiastic, but extremely vague, description. Nor does he plan to linger with her: he only allows himself an hour. He could have pocketed Ana's letter and never passed on the message to the Marquis; but part of the fun he is looking forward to is seeing Mota's face when the poor fool turns up at midnight ("mas yo bien sé que a las doce/harás mayores estremos", II, 372–3). His malicious jokes are directed against men as well as women. Having dishonoured Isabela, he has the effrontery to apologize to Octavio for having left Naples without saying goodbye. He is delighted with the success of his lie to Batricio and goes out of his way to deceive Aminta's father as well. He is witheringly contemptuous of his own father's tearful reproaches. He jeers at the epitaph of the old man he has killed. He mocks and plucks the statue's stone beard and defies the statue to fight him with its stone sword. The invitation to supper is a gibe.

Until his decision to keep his second appointment with the statue, each of Don Juan's exploits is carried out for fun, and the fun is always malicious. Furthermore he presumes that he will get away with it. In the short run he relies on his family connections – his uncle the ambassador, and his father, the King's right-hand man. In the long run, death is a long way away.

Until his surprising decision to keep his word to Don Gonzalo, almost everything the play has shown about the character of Don Juan is summed up in his title, "El Burlador". So far, he is very close to being a personification of malicious deceit. To the qualities of deceitfulness, flippancy and malice implied in the word "burlador" can be added the airy presumption of his catchphrase "¡Qué largo me lo fiáis!" This brings in his attitude towards the all-important matters of death and the hereafter. This attitude is completely in keeping with the rest but a new dimension has been added to his character. His invitation to the statue shows that he has no more respect for the dead than for the living. The range of his "burlas" has been extended, but he is still characterized by a set of closely allied moral qualities and by an appropriate tone of voice. Vividly presented though these have been, there is as yet very little more to him than this.

His decision to go to supper in the chapel produces what in drama and fiction is the right kind of surprise : a piece of behaviour which was not predictable but which, when it comes, can be seen to be perfectly credible and, what is more, illuminating. It is surprising that the Burlador should be so set upon keeping his word. Would it not have been more in character for him to snap his fingers at such an idea? Might we not have expected him to find it amusing to break this promise as he has broken others, and leave the statue to push scorpions round his plate all by himself? When he reminds Catalinón of his obligation ("¿No ves que di mi palabra?", III, 867) and Catalinón replies

> Y cuando se la quebrantes,
> ¿qué importa? ¿Ha de pedirte
> una figura de jaspe
> la palabra? (III, 868–71)

the two seem to have changed places. Don Juan's answer is even more astonishing :

Podrá el muerto
llamarme a voces infame. (III, 871–2)

Don Juan has already been provoked by the inscription's mention
of a traitor and by the statue's injunction not to be afraid. What
now emerges is that there is something which the Burlador takes
seriously to the point of madness: the necessity of never losing
face. To break his word now would look like cowardice. He is
mortally afraid of appearing afraid (2). The Burlador insists on
being a man of his word. As soon as this contradiction appears we
recognize its "rightness"; it produces the illusion that there has
been more to Don Juan's character all along. His insistence on
being a true "caballero" has other implications (see "Themes", below). From the point of view of characterization what is important
is that this unexpected piece of behaviour prevents the character
from being a simple abstraction. He has now become a walking
paradox.

We are still very far from knowing all about Don Juan Tenorio,
or rather from knowing all there would be to know were he a real
person. For obvious reasons, little is said about his physical attri-
butes. Is he tall or short? Dark or fair? Fat or thin? Should his lips
be full and sensual or thin and cruel? Should his voice be deep or
light? His movements sinuous and cat-like or sudden and bird-like?
All this will depend on the actor playing the part. But what about
his past – his childhood, his upbringing, his relationship with his
mother? Is he an only child? This is the sort of area in which a
psychoanalyst might look for explanations of Don Juan's psycho-
pathic lack of conscience. And yet we are given no information
whatever about his past beyond the fact that the escapade in Naples
is not the first of its kind (I, 77–86; II, 42–3). We may feel that we
can readily imagine his childhood, his behaviour towards his tutors
(there would surely have been several), his taste in clothes . . . In
fact, we have not been given enough information to fill in the simplest questionnaire. What the playwright has done is to create a
character from a small nucleus of allied moral qualities plus one
other which is unexpected. This combination is enough to create
the illusion – for illusion it is – that there is more to the character
than we can ever know.

It must be added that all these qualities are conveyed not only in
behaviour but in just the right tone of voice. As one would expect

of a "burlador", the tone is generally mocking. Even where it is not, the staccato commands and rejoinders, the transparent flattery, the bravado, the impatience and even the unflinching courage all seem to come from the same centre: disparagement of others and glorification of self. For Don Juan Tenorio nothing and nobody is worth taking seriously except Don Juan Tenorio.

As partial explanations of his extraordinary vitality I would offer two further suggestions taken from authorities in widely different fields. The first is from the psychiatrist Anthony Storr who, in his excellent book on *The Dynamics of Creation* (London, 1972), remarks that "we are often more moved by personifications of impulse than by real people" and explains that "that is because the impulses are really our own, whereas another person is always something 'other', as well as being more complicated than these images" (p. 184). With exactly the right degree of complication to be individual, Don Juan is just such a personification of impulses which are all too much our own: lust, aggression, vainglory, contempt for everything but self.

The second suggestion comes from further afield and concerns the phenomenon of hyper-reaction in young herring-gulls.[3] To induce their mother to regurgitate food for them, young herring-gulls tap on the under-side of their mother's bill where there is a red spot. They will tap with varying frequency on this spot even on the bills of two-dimensional models in un-gull-like shapes and colours; what is especially interesting for our purposes is that when presented with a pencil-shaped red rod adorned at the tip with three sharply-edged white bands they will tap more vigorously than on the bill of a three-dimensional model of their mother's head. An exaggeration of the sign stimuli of redness, contrast and thinness produces a stronger reaction than a more life-like model. Perhaps it is by a comparable process of isolation, simplification and exaggeration of sign stimuli that the playwright produces such a strong reaction in his audience. If so Don Juan Tenorio is what Tinbergen and Perdeck would call a "supernormal dummy". In reacting to him more intensely than if he were a likeness of a real person, we are all the playwright's gulls.

[3] See N. Tinbergen and A. C. Perdeck, "On the Stimulus Situation Releasing the Begging Response in the Newly Hatched Herring Gull Chick (*Larus argentatus pont.*)", *Behaviour*, III (1950), 1-38.

None of the other parts is anything like so important as Don Juan's, but each of them has some individuality. Collectively they suggest a general view of humanity, or at least of society.[4]

Isabela

Isabela makes only four short appearances, during two of which she hardly speaks. In the opening scene the audience share her bewilderment at discovering that she has been deceived. Her part here is limited to ladylike exclamations of delight, alarm and dismay.[5] In her second scene the King bombards her with questions which he gives her no time to answer. Only her exit-lines are at all distinctive. They reveal beneath her conventional distress a cool assessment of her prospects:

> mas no será el yerro tanto
> si el duque Octavio lo enmienda. (I, 189–90)

She is prepared to let it be thought that her offender was Octavio if it means that Octavio will have to marry her. It is also worth noting that, although Don Juan deceived her, her own behaviour would have been just as dishonourable if the visitor to her bedroom had been the man she took him for.

At her next appearance, when it seems that she will have to marry Don Juan instead, she tells Fabio that her only regret is that she will not thereby recover her lost reputation (III, 331–6). When she meets Tisbea, the Duchess and the fishergirl join together in lamenting the fate of any woman who trusts men. Isabela's last aside is cryptic (the text of this whole scene is garbled): she invites Tisbea to travel with her, adding that this will assist her own revenge (III, 406–7). Perhaps this means that she hopes Don Juan will be forced to marry Tisbea and that she herself will then be able to marry Octavio after all. However that may be, in the final scene, after the news of Don Juan's death has been brought in, she makes no reply to Octavio's offer of marriage. Presumably she accepts his

---

[4] For a study of this aspect readers are referred to a forthcoming article by J. E. Varey on "Social Criticism in *El burlador de Sevilla*" to be published in *Theatre Research International*. Professor Varey kindly let me see his article at a late stage in the preparation of this Guide. As a result I have made some modifications although on many points we had reached similar conclusions independently.

[5] For some interesting further possibilities see *20*.

hand in silence. She has never expressed any feelings for him apart from her initial delight at having (as she thought) caught her man. Apart from her title, her beauty and a belated concern with her reputation, Don Juan's most socially exalted victim has not much to recommend her.

Octavio

Compared with Don Juan, Octavio is a conventionally honourable "caballero". But he is no idealist. He does not spring to his lady's defence. He gladly accepts an alternative bride unseen. He accepts an offer of escape from the man sent by his sovereign to arrest him. He will not fight a duel if the King of Castile forbids it. He curtly offers to marry Isabela when everybody present knows that she is not a virgin. Like Don Juan's other victims, he is presented ironically.

When he first appears he is the traditionally sleepless distracted lover, pacing up and down on sentry-go before the castle of his honour. At the line "pensamientos de Isabela" (I, 203) the audience can guess who he is. From then on, they can view him ironically, as they know what has been happening to Isabela and Octavio does not. The by-play with the servant who suggests that Octavio's sufferings are self-imposed probably has more to do with dramatic irony than with characterization: the audience know that there *is* now something to prevent the marriage. But Octavio's insistence that, even when they love each other, courtship between a duke and a duchess is not so simple as between a lackey and a washerwoman indicates a concern with correct social forms. Confronted with Don Pedro's false accusations, Octavio is stunned by the news of how Isabela has betrayed him, but he is quick to believe the worst:

> que la mujer más constante
> es, en efeto, mujer. (I, 357–8)

Rather than try to clear himself of a false charge, he accepts Don Pedro's devious offer of a chance to flee the country.

When he appears before the King of Castile to lodge his complaint, he jumps at the chance to marry a well-bred *sevillana* instead. When he discovers who the offender was, and seeks the King's permission to challenge Don Juan to a duel, he tamely accepts the King's refusal. He also accepts without question the order that he should marry next day.

When Aminta comes to court in pursuit of Don Juan, Octavio sees his chance of revenge. Presumably his plan is to produce Aminta at Don Juan's and Isabela's spousals, thereby preventing their marriage. This plan is forestalled by Don Juan's death. Octavio abruptly, and without any show of emotion, offers to marry the "widowed" Isabela. She, as we have seen, receives his offer in silence. There is little reason for enthusiasm on either side.

The King of Naples

He appears overworked and confused, rapping out questions and not waiting for the answers. He wants the scandal in his palace discreetly investigated and, if possible, hushed up. If the intruder turns out to be Duke Octavio, then the Duke must be secretly arrested and forced to marry Isabela. The King's trust in the Spanish ambassador is shown to be misplaced. He seems to represent hard-pressed and fallible authority doing its best.

Don Pedro Tenorio

His is the most colourful of the minor parts. The first deception shown in full in this play is carried out not by the Burlador but by his uncle. Ordered to arrest the unknown intruder, Don Pedro discovers that the young man is his own nephew. Scandalized and at the same time terrified lest the scandal should come out, Don Pedro realizes that he will have to use his wits ("Industria me ha de valer", I, 75). He is angry at being placed in such a delicate situation and delivers his nephew a lecture (I, 77–93) – the sort of futile homily that weak authority falls back on, and that tells any experienced miscreant that he is going to be let off. But now they have no time to lose ("*Nos* daña la dilación" – they are both at risk). With a timely reminder that they are blood-relations, Don Juan kneels down in histrionic submission and surrenders his sword. Touched by such humility (not to mention his own shrewd self-interest) the uncle lets him go. When the King comes back to see that his orders have been carried out Don Pedro launches into a vivid circumstantial account, complete with gestures and mimicry, of a scene which never took place. No sooner had the King given his orders, he says, than the intruder drew his sword, flung his cloak over his arm, so (the old diplomat demonstrates), and fought himself free. He leapt over the balcony and they found him writhing at the foot of the wall "like a coiled snake" (I, 126–40). In seconds he was up and as the soldiers moved in for the kill (here Don Pedro imitates their shouts), the bloodstained figure left them blinking. The audience know that all this is pure fiction.

In his scene with Octavio, Don Pedro is equally devious and adds fresh detail and some rhetorical flourishes to his lies. His first remarks are quizzical if not sarcastic, for Octavio is not sleeping soundly, but is up and about suspiciously early. Is Don Pedro pretending to see signs of guilt in the man he knows to be innocent? Or is he wondering could the mysterious intruder have been Octavio after all? Whichever it is, he then embarks on another of his colourful false reports. In the dark hour before the dawn, when the black giants of the night were folding up their tents, the carved ceilings of the palace reverberated with a woman's screams. (So far, his story is true, but the manner is that of a practised storyteller.) The man he was sent to arrest was the devil incarnate, gave him the slip and vanished among the elms near the castle walls. "Esos olmos": details like this lend conviction to a lie. Now, he tells the Duke, Isabela is accusing – Octavio! The Duke can hardly believe his ears. The Ambassador protests with a string of rhetorical assurances: as there are birds in the air and fish in the sea, as a true friend is loyal and an enemy false[!] ... The Duke is ready to believe him, for the most faithful woman is, after all, only a woman. Happy to have him think so, Don Pedro offers the chance of escape to the second man he has been sent to arrest. Octavio's flight will seem to confirm his guilt.

Like his uncle, Don Juan lends conviction to his lies with telling detail (he promises Aminta shoes with *linings* of *beaten* silver and *nails* of Tíbar gold – little luxuries that wouldn't even show, but just make her *feel* rich – and rings set with *"trasparentes* perlas *finas"*, III, 288–96). "Mozo soy y mozo fuiste", he tells his uncle before surrendering (I, 62). Deceitfulness runs in the family. It seems not too fanciful to see Don

Pedro as resembling what Don Juan might have become had he
lived. A deceived deceiver, Don Pedro Tenorio is not a credit to
his caste.

Don Diego Tenorio

Don Diego's behaviour, by comparison, is correct and loyal.
When he arrests another man for a crime committed by Don
Juan, he does so, unlike his brother, in good faith. There is
nevertheless a strong indication that because his father is the
King's favourite Don Juan receives – and expects – more indul-
gence than he deserves. The first time Don Diego appears he is
shown begging the King not to allow a duel between Octavio and
Don Juan. The King quite understands Don Diego's motive
("honor de padre"), although it is difficult to see how the father's
honour would suffer if Don Juan were to fight and win. The
King also says that it is only thanks to the royal regard for Don
Diego that Don Juan is to be let off with banishment to Lebrija.
When Octavio comes to ask to be allowed to challenge Don Juan,
both Don Diego and the King know very well that Don Juan is
guilty of the offence of which Octavio accuses him. And yet Don
Diego will not hear his son called a traitor. The King reprimands
him for putting his hand to his sword in the royal presence, but
goes on to side with him, and to insist that Octavio respect Don
Juan. This is patently unjust.

Don Diego severely reprimands his son and warns him of
divine retribution, but he himself will not punish him (7). Indeed
he says he can do nothing with him:

> Pues no te vence castigo
> con cuanto hago y cuanto digo,
> a Dios tu castigo dejo. (II, 423–5)

When all Don Juan's misdeeds are finally made known and the
King orders his arrest and execution, Don Diego goes so far as
to urge the King to see that the sentence is carried out. This and
the King's exclamation, "¡Esto mis privados hacen!" suggest
that both the King and his favourite have learnt their lesson;
which implies that they both had a lesson to learn.

Mota

The Marquis is first shown greeting Don Juan as a long-lost friend. They have a good deal in common. He brings Don Juan up to date with news of the prostitutes well known to them both. Like Don Juan (and, incidentally, like another young aristocrat Don Pedro de Esquivel) he is fond of playing the "perro muerto" trick on them. This and the cruel verbal jokes at the ageing whores' expense show the contemptuous callousness of these young men. This is incidental comedy, but it is not irrelevant, for the "perro muerto" can stand as the type of all Don Juan's "burlas" against women. What, after all, is seducing duchesses and country girls with promises of marriage but another form of cheating whores of their fee?

Mota is one of Don Juan's male victims, but he himself is just as fond of this form of amusement. Even in the middle of his excitement over Ana's invitation he takes pleasure in the thought of deceiving Beatriz. Had he been able to keep his appointment with Ana and been discovered by her father, we do not know how he might have behaved; but we know he fully intended to take up her offer. In the final scene he is understandably relieved to hear that Ana saw through Don Juan's deception in time. Neither the audience nor the other characters are bound to believe this (even though Don Juan tells the statue the same thing, III, 963–4). If it is true, the Marquis and his cousin seem to have been let off rather lightly. He is certainly not a model "galán". On the contrary, he is presented, with some asperity, as a callous young nobleman with a double standard of sexual morality.

Ana

Ana never in fact appears. Presumably her tiny off-stage part was doubled with one of the other "damas". She does, however, write a letter to Mota which (presumably) her maid delivers into the hands of a complete stranger. That Don Juan is not the man she invites should not obscure the fact that, in the decorous language of a damsel in distress, she is offering herself to a brothel-creeper. As things turn out, she has to marry him first. But what her father says to Don Juan goes for her too:

No importa, que ya pusiste
tu intento. (III, 965–6)

She and the Marquis seem more blameworthy and less unlucky
than Octavio and Isabela. But none of these aristocratic victims
is a model of virtue.

Don Gonzalo

Don Gonzalo talks more like a statue before he becomes one.
On his early appearances he is stiffly conventional. He makes a
brief report on his diplomatic mission to Lisbon and gives a
guidebook description of the city's assets.[6] He accepts the King's
offer of a marriage for his daughter without even knowing who
the husband is to be. On hearing Ana's screams he shows more
concern for the family's reputation than for what may be happening to her. Threatened by Don Juan, he stands his ground and
makes the first lunge ("¡Muere, traidor!" II, 533). He dies swear-
ing revenge on such a cowardly attacker. Apart from the Lisbon
speech, which has little to do with characterization or even with
the plot, his part so far contains nothing at all distinctive. Like
Don Juan's other victims he is presented to some extent ironically, in that when he accepts Don Juan Tenorio as a son-in-law
(I, 873–4) the audience knows so much more than he does. By
the time he is shown dying in an attempt to avenge the family
honour the audience have heard the contents of his daughter's
letter to Mota and know that he is dying for a lost cause. In Golden-
Age drama the words of dying men are usually weighted with
special significance. Don Juan does not hear Don Gonzalo's last
words ("Seguiráte mi furor", II, 542), but the audience do. They
cannot yet be expected to guess how the threat will be carried
out; but when they hear Don Juan's oath to Aminta, watch him
scoff at Don Gonzalo's epitaph and hear his crazy assertion
that the dead man may publicly denounce him, they will sense,
however vaguely, that a prophecy is coming true. If Don Juan's
fatal decision is taken to be a case of hubris (*10*) Don Gonzalo's
threat of avenging fury may be seen to be carried out to the letter.

---

[6] For a more favourable view of the Lisbon speech see *18*.

The statue

The "barba" (or, specialist in old man's parts) of the company
has a much bigger opportunity when he comes back as the
"convidado de piedra". In the first supper scene he does not have
much to say, but his entrance is excitingly prepared for by the
ominous knocking and by the terror of Catalinón and the other
servants who dare not open the door. Confronted by Don Juan,
the statue introduces himself with laconic dignity. He does not
speak again until he and Don Juan are alone. By this time the
comic terror of Catalinón and the nervy bravado of Don Juan
have built up further expectations. Again his few lines are simple
and formal. His exit is slow and impressive. By the second supper
scene, tension and expectancy have been heightened even further.
As before, his words are grave and simple, but there is an
occasional hint of mockery:

> No entendí que me cumplieras
> la palabra, según haces
> de todos burla. (III, 889–91)
>
> Valiente estás. (III, 906)

Without any of Don Juan's ostentation, he leads his victim on.
Because he does not confide in the audience, they will not be sure
what to expect. He remains mysterious until after Don Juan's cry
of pain. Once he has his victim in his grasp he makes himself
tremendously explicit:

> Las maravillas de Dios
> son, don Juan, investigables,
> y así quiere que tus culpas
> a manos de un muerto pagues,
> y si pagas desta suerte,
> ésta es justicia de Dios:
> "quien tal hace, que tal pague". (III, 952–8)

This last line was the traditional refrain of the town-crier when
crimes and sentences were proclaimed at public floggings and
executions. Its use here transforms the statue into a "Pregonero
de Dios" and the scene into a public execution "a lo divino". The

climax comes when Don Juan asks for a confessor (which the prisoner at an ordinary execution would have been allowed). Don Gonzalo answers with the single terrible line "No hay lugar; ya acuerdas tarde".

One can hardly speak of "character" in discussing the statue's role. A mysterious but by no means unearthly figure, he emerges at last as the agent of divine justice.

Alfonso XI of Castile

Like his counterpart in Naples, King Alfonso does his best to clear up the confusion created by Don Juan. He is always at least one step behind, and seen by the audience to be so. When he decides that Don Juan shall marry Ana, the audience know about Isabela and King Alfonso does not. As soon as he hears about the Naples affair he adjusts his plans. Don Juan must marry Isabela and Don Gonzalo can be placated by being given a post in the royal household. The audience by this time know about Tisbea. When Octavio arrives, the King knows that Don Juan has offended the Duke; but rather than revealing what he knows or offering to punish the offender, he hastily placates the Duke by offering him Ana's hand in marriage. After Don Gonzalo's murder he summarily orders the execution of the wrong man. It is true that the evidence points to Mota's guilt, and also that minor characters are often given very perfunctory treatment by Golden-Age playwrights, but even allowing for this, King Alfonso seems to be presented as a rather hasty pragmatist. He is ready to reprieve Mota simply because the orphaned Ana needs a husband (to marry her off to her father's murderer, even at her own request, seems an improbable choice). He chooses a husband for Don Gonzalo's daughter when, a moment before, he has had to ask whether the ambassador has any children. He yields to Don Diego's pressure to protect Don Juan from Octavio. When at last he sentences Don Juan, the audience know that the Burlador is already dead. The best the King can do then is to direct that the survivors marry each other.

The playwright does not appear to show much confidence in either of his kings. Nor is his picture of the aristocracy at all flattering. What about the "villanos"?

Tisbea

Far from the intrigues of the Neapolitan court, enter a girl with a fishing-rod who talks in elaborate courtly language of sapphire seas and sparkling sands, of the cooing of rock-doves and the lapping of waves, and of her own blessed immunity to love. The splendour and preciosity of her language are in striking contrast to her humble station; the sensuousness of her response to her surroundings seems at odds with her professed freedom from desire (*11*). The Latin poet Horace begins his Second Epode (the favourite classical model for Renaissance and later poems in praise of the simple life) with the words "Beatus ille" (Happy the man). The early part of Tisbea's speech is a kind of "Beata illa" (cf. I, 416, "Dichosa yo mil veces") in praise of life by the seashore – except that, being spoken by the lucky one herself, its tone is not wistful but complacent. This girl is pleased with herself. Her attitude to her love-lorn admirers and to the silly little fishes seems to be much the same. It is significant also that she describes the sinking ship in terms of humbled pride. A Golden-Age audience, used to seeing stage accidents and disasters as omens and symbols, would probably have sensed in the wreck of the proud vessel a premonition of the wreck of the proud beauty – at least when they discovered who had been on board.

Left alone with the unconscious Don Juan, whom she knows by now to be the son of the Lord Chamberlain (I, 570–2), the haughty Tisbea cradles his head in her lap with mingled tenderness and awe:

> Mancebo, excelente,
> gallardo, noble y galán.
> Volved en vos, caballero. (I, 579–81)

Her tone changes as soon as he comes round. Her pert reply to Don Juan's question ("¿Dónde estoy? – Ya podéis ver: / en brazos de una mujer", I, 582–3) is like an echo of Don Juan's own insolent answer to the King (I, 22–3). Her response to his lyrical "piropos" is, to begin with, teasingly sceptical. She mocks his lyrical conceits with ironical conceits of her own. Her remark about salt and her play on the proverbial expression "si en seco

hago esto, ¿qué hiciera en mojado?" are more earthy than her
earlier poetic speech. She makes much of Don Juan's promise of
fire, yet he himself has said nothing about fire. The fire must be
in his looks and in her own body. For all that he is cold and wet
they are burning for each other. How she has changed! The
fishermen's fulsome compliments had never interested her before.
Now she is pleasurably aware of her own physical attractiveness.
After Don Juan's asides to Catalinón he reverts to his role of
suffering lover. She is still playfully incredulous. But if she sees
that his protestations are all talk, she knows very well what he
is talking about. When she first came on, Tisbea was revelling in
her own invulnerability. Now she is enjoying a dangerous game.

When she and Don Juan meet again, the passionate avowals
come from her. It is his turn to lead his quarry on by pretending
not to believe her. As soon as she has declared herself, Don Juan
promises to marry her. She has not asked for this and hesitates
to believe him. Only after a further lyrical declaration does Tisbea
make marriage a condition of her surrender. When Don Juan
renews his promise in the face of her portentous warning, Tisbea,
who not long ago had been glorying in her role of "mujer
esquiva",[7] or man-shy tormentress, now promises lubriciously to
make his offer worth his while. "¿Por dónde tengo de entrar? –
Ven y te diré por dónde " (I, 955–6). It would do no harm if this
exchange brought a guffaw from somewhere in the audience. The
whole scene is as daring a display of mutual lust as the slobbery
supper-scene in the film of *Tom Jones*.

Tisbea calls down the wrath of heaven on Don Juan if he does
not keep his word. Yet by this time she may not be much more
serious than he is: the line could be spoken provocatively, even
with a giggle. Tisbea's intimations of mortality and divine punishment may be no more than the regressive nursery moralizing of
the flirt.

"¡Fuego, fuego, que me quemo . . .!": even though her downfall was predictable, the elemental violence of her next speech
comes as a shock. Her shame and fury defy rational analysis as

---

[7] On this aspect of Tisbea see Melveena McKendrick, *Woman and Society in
the Spanish Drama of the Golden Age: a study of the "mujer varonil"* (Cambridge, 1974), pp. 158-9.

her ravings veer wildly between the figurative and the literal (see Chapter 5). She even makes a crazy identification between her house and herself – calling down fiery meteorites to set alight the cabin's windswept "hair". All this is love's revenge on one who had mocked his power and the sufferings of his victims. Like the doomed ship and the windswept cottage, the stolen horses probably have a symbolic as well as a literal value. In Golden-Age drama runaway horses are recognized symbols of uncontrolled appetites. Tisbea herself bred the mare on which Don Juan rode away. Tisbea's latent passion made her betrayal possible. While the demented girl plunges into the sea from whence love's retribution came, one of the fishermen makes the choric comment that such is the fate of pride.

Although she speaks of herself as a "burladora burlada" (I, 1013–16), her later appearances show that her vindictive fury has not been assuaged, nor her pride humbled. She continues to rail against the sea, as Isabela rails against the darkness. Then, with only slightly more self-knowledge, they both lament the fate of any woman who trusts men. The text of the scene appears to be garbled, but the drift is plain: as the gales have destroyed Tisbea's home so she herself was carried away by passion.

Tisbea's "culto" language may be partly prompted by literary fashion; it is also probably connected with her pride. Tirso's "villanas" usually speak with an earthy popular directness (cf. *Antona García* or *Mari-Hernández la gallega*); but then they are usually representatives of a wholesome rustic innocence.[8] Like Don Juan's other victims, Tisbea is far from innocent.

Aminta

Aminta is the least blameworthy of all Don Juan's victims. The worst that can be said of her is that she is naively credulous, dazzled as she is by the sudden prospect of a brilliant marriage. In her first scene she is given little to do but look pretty. In her second she appears genuinely distressed and indignant at the way the strange "caballero" has upset her husband and spoilt their wedding. Her words give no hint that she feels attracted to

[8] See C. A. Jones, "Tirso de Molina and Country Life", *Philological Quarterly*, LI (1972), 197-204.

this brazen intruder. In view of what soon happens, an actress might contrive to suggest that Aminta protests too much.[9] Ironical or not, her indignant exclamation that "La desvergüenza en España/se ha hecho caballería" (III, 131–2) expresses one of the most important social comments in the play (see "Themes", below).

When Don Juan approaches her bedroom, she thinks, understandably, that it is Batricio who is calling her. This time Don Juan does not attempt to pass himself off as the man his victim is expecting. Instead, he invites Aminta to take a good look at him ("Mira/ de espacio, Aminta, quién soy", III, 204–5). Perhaps he has sensed that Aminta is already attracted towards him against her will. At any rate he is counting on being able to dazzle the simple country girl with his fine clothes and fine manners, and by offering her the prospect of becoming a lady. He disarms her would-be heroic resistance by flattering her complexion, and by announcing that he is already her husband. Aminta's instincts tell her to mistrust his "retóricas mentiras", but the news of her repudiation by Batricio is too much for her. In confirmation of his promise of marriage she exacts from Don Juan an impressive-sounding pledge. Abandoned by her father and her husband-to-be, she is a victim of their credulity as much as of her own. In the short scenes after she has been deceived, she is presented as a country girl at Court, a naive figure of fun.

Batricio

Full of forebodings from the moment Don Juan's arrival is announced (II, 671–3), Batricio, even more than Octavio, is ready to believe the worst of the woman he loves ("Al fin, al fin es mujer", III, 68). As soon as Don Juan claims to have dishonoured her (III, 63) – and Batricio finishes his sentence for him – Batricio wants no more to do with her. An audience might have some sympathy with the rueful account of the way the poor bumpkin has been imposed upon (III, 1–52), but his resentment is expressed in comic terms. Compared with Lope's *Peribáñez* or the people of *Fuenteovejuna*, he is decidedly weak-kneed. At the end of the play he, like Octavio, agrees to marry one of Don Juan's dishonoured relicts.

[9] On possible ambiguities in this scene see 22.

Gaseno

Like Batricio and Aminta, Gaseno is presented in a comic light. His willingness to extend his hospitality to all comers ("Venga el Coloso de Rodas . . .", II, 683 ff) is made to look foolish,[10] as is his ready acceptance of Don Juan as a son-in-law and his later assertion that "Doña Aminta es muy honrada" (III, 801). Proud of his prosperity, and of being a *cristiano viejo* (III, 803–5), he has none of the shrewdness and none of the dignity of a *Villano en su rincón* or an *Alcalde de Zalamea*. This play holds out no hope that sound peasant stock will make good the deficiencies of the nobility.

Catalinón

Part of Catalinón's role is the routine comedy of the "gracioso": his invective against sea-water, his scatological jokes, his promise not to reveal his master's identity when he has just done so (I, 681–4; cf. I, 570–8). His main comic contribution is his exaggerated fright in the scenes with the statue, which effectively adds to the tension rather than relieving it. His more serious function is to voice forebodings and issue warnings, and finally to come on like the messenger in a Greek tragedy with news of the hero's death. His warnings and forebodings both prepare the audience for the climax and reveal, through his master's increasingly violent reactions, Don Juan's mounting anxiety. Conventionally, the comic servant was always cowardly where his master was heroic. In many of the more serious *comedias*, however (*El caballero de Olmedo* and *El médico de su honra* are outstanding examples), the "gracioso" is made to appear in some ways wiser than the hero. Catalinón's fears turn out to be well-founded and his master's confidence misplaced.

The more one looks at Don Juan's victims, both individually and collectively, the less impressive do his conquests become (6).

[10] Competition in wedding celebrations is still a point of honour in rural Spain. See Carmelo Lisón Tolosana, *Belmonte de los Caballeros: a sociological study of a Spanish town* (Oxford, 1966), p. 322. It may not be only the nobles' false sense of honour that the playwright is denouncing.

Not only the girls – a duchess out to marry her man at any price, a reckless young *sevillana* ready to risk disgrace to her noble family, a conceited fisher-girl and a country bride with ideas above her station – but their menfolk and even their kings all play into his hands. Amongst all these worldly aristocrats, impetuous young ladies, pretentious peasants and harassed heads of state only two figures seem to be beyond – or almost beyond – reproach. One is a stone effigy and the other is a clown.[11]

[11] Ter Horst (*18*) and Varey (see note 4 above) have helped me to see that the playwright's disillusionment is not so complete as I had supposed: the Lisbon speech offers a vision of a less corrupt society. But this only darkens the rest of the picture.

5 *Imagery*

Following a trend begun by critics of Shakespeare in the 1930s a number of critics of Spanish drama have come to recognize that a play can be a kind of poem, held together by threads of metaphor. The metaphorical language used by the characters can link separate events of the action not only to each other but to the ideas which constitute the theme. A neat summary of how this is done in *El burlador* can be found in a recent essay by Bruce Wardropper (*28*). "In *El burlador de Sevilla*," he says, "dramatized metaphor, pervasive irony, and poetic theme join forces to give a disjointed play its intrinsic unity."

Some of the recurring images which contribute to this unity have been studied in detail. Joaquín Casalduero (*1*) long ago noted how the oaths and warnings of divine punishment become more and more explicit. Heinrich Bihler (*9*) draws attention to the repeated outbreaks of fire — Tisbea's cabin, the torches after Don Gonzalo's murder, the scene in the chapel. In my own essay (*10*) I mentioned the repetition of the handclasp (both in words and action), the metaphorical references to heaven and hell and to souls in torment as well as to burning; also the recurring ideas of keeping promises, destroying or pursuing reputations, abusing hospitality. To these can be added the idea of tricking someone by exploiting their sense of honour. Brian Morris has made a fuller study of "Metaphor in *El burlador de Sevilla*" (*11*). He notes the repeated references to the destruction of buildings as well as to fire. Tisbea is rock-like in her resistance to her admirers ("a sus promesas, roca"), but "amor abrasa peñas". The thatch of her cottage is straw to wrap up her honour, but straw soon catches fire. She is immune to the "asp" of love but has her foot bitten by a "viper". Don Juan's uncle once described him as writhing like a coiled snake; Don Juan is made to eat snakes. Don Juan burns with desire for white hands; he is burnt by the white[?] hand of the statue. He is a giant defying heaven; a dead man may fell a giant with one blow. He is a cloud; he snuffs out lights; he is a

creature of the night.[1] "Tirso", Morris concludes, "does not let
the metaphors he chooses, not even those as stereotyped as *sol*
and Troy, stiffen into lifelessness but makes them supple and
suggestive, giving them a point and a purpose." One can go
further and say that he brings dead metaphors to life.

This is particularly true of the metaphors used in the episode
with Tisbea. In seventeenth-century poetry storms and shipwrecks
were long-familiar metaphors for the torments of love. Don Juan
deftly applies them to his present situation (I, 584–96). From the
sea's raging hell he has emerged into a serene heaven. The storm
has cast him up at Tisbea's feet; he has come safe into harbour;
in the dawn of her divine beauty he is born again. Fresh from a
real shipwreck, he might almost be offering up thanks to the Star
of the Sea. And so perhaps he should be. The nautical-cum-
religious language of petrarchan love (cf. p. 24 above) is for those
who are not drowning but waving.

In his second scene with Tisbea, Don Juan speaks of offering
up his life in her service (I, 925–7), of her hair ensnaring his
soul (I, 938–9), of being her lifelong slave (I, 945–6), and of how
her consent to marry him brings glory to his soul (I, 957). The
blasphemies of courtly love are doubly ironic now that God and
death have been invoked to seal a promise which is patently
insincere: Don Juan does not mean what he is saying; at the
same time his words mean more than he knows.

The whole Tisbea episode is rich in metaphor. Her appearance
"con una caña de pescar en la mano" closely follows Octavio's
exclamations on the frailty of women: "¡Ah veleta! ¡Débil caña!"
(I, 369).[2] Tisbea's conceit about the peacock's tail and the sail of
the sinking ship is, as we have seen, suggestive of her own pride
before her fall. Underlying all the conceits about fire and water
there may be a distant recollection of the birth of Venus from

[1] For a structuralist study of the imagery of light and darkness see M. Durán
and R. González Echevarría, "Luz y oscuridad: la estructura simbólica de *El
burlador de Sevilla*", in *Homenaje a William L. Fichter*, ed. A. David Kossoff and
José Amor y Vázquez (Madrid, 1971), pp. 201-9. J. E. Varey (see note 4 to ch. 4)
sees the candle in Naples and the torches in Seville as symbolic of the relative concern for truth in the two kingdoms.

[2] I owe this observation to Dr Michael D. McGaha of Pomona College, Clare-
mont, California, whose article "In defense of ¿*Tan largo me lo fiáis?*" is soon
to appear in the *Bulletin of the Comediantes*.

the sea.[3] The wind, the waves, the storm-cloud and the down-pour are all, like the flames and the galloping horses, associated with Tisbea's unruly passions. Tisbea has been betrayed not only by Don Juan but also by her own passionate nature.

The repeated allusions to Troy are mentioned by Duncan Moir (25) in connection with the Tisbea episode in which most of them occur. First Don Juan rescuing Catalinón from the sea is com-pared to Aeneas rescuing his father from the burning city (I, 502–3). Then Tisbea herself compares Don Juan to the wooden horse because she senses that he is more dangerous than he seems (I, 613–16). Don Juan tells Catalinón that he plans to do to Tisbea what Aeneas did to Dido (I, 899–900). Finally Tisbea laments that

> Mi pobre edificio queda
> hecho otra Troya en las llamas. (I, 989–90)

There are two other references to Troy. Mota, seeing the torches of the party coming to investigate the murder of Don Gonzalo, compares the flames to "una Troya que se abrasa" (II, 576); and Don Juan himself is known, according to his father, as the Hector of Seville (II, 42). Probably one should not read very much into these references, all of which were commonplaces. There is per-haps some irony in the way the man Tisbea first sees as Aeneas because of his unselfish heroism later sees himself as Aeneas in a less creditable role. It may be relevant to remember that Aeneas was the son of Venus. The link between the "Greek horse" and Tisbea's own downfall is obvious enough. The Marquis probably means simply that the whole city seems to be on fire; but these flames too are the result of unlawful passion. As for Don Juan's being compared with Hector, the stay or prop of Troy, the choice of this particular hero (a dignified and respectable family man) seems singularly unsuitable. Perhaps it is significant that Hector was chiefly remembered as a defeated hero.[4] Perhaps the play-

[3] See the delightful essay "El nacimiento de don Juan" by Pedro Salinas, in *Ensayos de literatura hispánica* (Madrid, 1967), pp. 158-67. For a Jungian ap-proach to the imagery see 22.

[4] Don Alonso, *El caballero de Olmedo*, is compared to Hector, Adonis and Leander, all of whom came to untimely ends. Ter Horst (*18* and *21*) points out that the epithet most commonly applied to Hector in classical times was "man-killer". This fits in well with the idea of Don Juan as a debased hero.

wright was seeking to endow the events of his play with an epic grandeur. More probably the effect of all the classical references is the same as that of Aminta's assertion that there are Emilias and Lucretias in the village of Dos Hermanas. Aminta is no Lucrece or Emily; the seduction of Tisbea will not launch a thousand ships; Don Juan is no Hector or Aeneas (except in perfidy). Heroes and heroines are not what they were.

The most insistently repeated metaphor in the play is such a dead one that we may hardly recognize it as a metaphor at all : the idea of "paying" for one's actions, or "repaying" someone else's. Don Juan has behaved ungratefully towards the kingdom (Naples) which took him in "atendiendo / que el haberte recibido / *pagaras* agradecido" (I, 89–91). He repays Tisbea's hospitality by deceiving her ("¡buen pago / a su hospedaje deseas!", I, 897–8; "Harto bien / te pagamos la posada", I, 911–12; "pagándole el hospedaje / en moneda de rigor", III, 612–13; "dile vida y hospedaje / y pagóme esta amistad / con mentirme y engañarme", III, 1002–4). And this after Tisbea had so unstintingly paid him for his promise to marry her ("No seré en pagarte esquiva", I, 948)! The trick attempted on Ana proves costly ("cara la burla ha costado", II, 555) and Mota will have to pay for it : "Yo, Don Juan, lo pagaré" (II, 556). Don Juan owes Aminta a debt of honour which (she hopes) he will not refuse to pay ("me debe el honor / y es noble y no ha de negarme", III, 1011–12). Payment is thus mentioned in connection with each of the four *burlas*. Don Diego too has had a poor return ("¡Ay, hijo! ¡Qué mal me pagas / el amor que te he tenido!" III, 783–4). At last he comes round to the view that as a reward for his own services his son should pay for all he has done :

> En premio de mis servicios
> haz que le prendan y pague
> sus culpas. (III, 1024–6)

As early as Act I, 901–3 Catalinón foresaw that Don Juan would have to pay for his deceptions with his life :

> Los que fingís y engañáis
> a las mujeres de esa suerte
> lo pagaréis con la muerte.

This provokes Don Juan's famous catchphrase "¡Qué largo me lo fiáis!" which introduces the idea of deferred payment on which Don Juan's whole attitude to morality is based: morality can wait. His refrain is eventually answered by the words of the singers in the chapel:

> no hay plazo que no llegue
> ni deuda que no se pague. (III, 932–3)

and finally by the statue:

> Quien tal hace que tal pague. (III, 974)

Don Juan's provocation of God and God's response to provocation are alike presented in terms of a financial transaction. Such metaphors go back at least as far as the New Testament. Instead of a Prodigal who "wasted his substance in riotous living" this play shows us one who lives riotously on the never-never. Rather than the wages of sin, death in this play is shown to be the price.

This financial imagery is not very subtle. On the contrary it is a heavy underlining of the play's "emphatic message" that "justice will be done" (24, p. 125). As for the other patterns of imagery, one can enjoy the play without being aware of them (as one can enjoy a piece of music without noticing, say, that one phrase in it is the inversion of another); even when they are recognized one need not believe that the playwright himself was aware of them. They can still contribute to the effectiveness of a play about sin and retribution.

One special feature of the play's poetry which cannot have been unconscious is the use of refrains. Eight scenes are rounded off by the repetition of a line spoken earlier in the same scene. These refrains are: Octavio's "¿con Isabela / hombre en palacio? Estoy loco" (I, 343–4, 373–4); Tisbea's "¡Plega a Dios que no mintáis!" (I, 620, 636, 696); Don Juan's "¡Qué largo me lo fiáis!" (I, 904, 944, 960); Tisbea's "¡Fuego, zagales, fuego, agua, agua! / ¡Amor, clemancia, que se abrasa el alma!" (I, 997–8, 1011–12, 1029–30, 1043–4); Don Juan's variant "tan largo me lo guardáis" (III, 120); Isabela's and Tisbea's "¡Mal haya la mujer que en hombres fía!" (III, 394, 402, 408); Don Juan's "tan largo me lo fiáis" (III, 473); the statue's "Esta es justicia de Dios: / quien tal hace, que tal pague" (III, 957–8, 973–4) repeated again by Catalinón at III, 1050. Lope de Vega in his *Arte nuevo* had recognized the value of a striking exit line:

> Remátense las escenas con sentencia,
> con donaire, con versos elegantes,
> de suerte que al entrarse el que recita,
> no deje con disgusto al auditorio. (p. 402)

Repeating an earlier line is one way of achieving this. Tirso de Molina elsewhere makes use of repeated catchphrases for comic effect (e.g. *El melancólico*, ends of Acts I and II.[5] *El amor médico*, 2014–15, 2030–1, 2082; 2981–2, 3001–2, 3121–2).[6] The serious use of refrains in *El burlador* is probably not unique, but it is unusual. It adds considerably to the effectiveness of "this awesome echo-chamber of a play" (*10*).

[5] Tirso de Molina, *Obras dramáticas completas*, ed. Blanca de los Ríos, I (Madrid, 1946), pp. 233, 248.

[6] Tirso de Molina, *Comedias*, II, ed. A. Zamora Vicente and M. J. Canellada de Zamora (Malrid, Clásicos Castellanos, 1947), pp. 82, 83, 85, 118, 119, 123.

6 *Themes*

Justice

The general theme can be summed up in the statue's words at the climax:

> Esta es justicia de Dios:
> "quien tal hace que tal pague".

Since the reward of virtue is not shown, all the emphasis here is on the punishment of vice. As we have seen, the vices which chiefly distinguish Don Juan are deceitfulness, flippancy, malice and presumption. Each of these vices can be seen to be fittingly punished in the way Don Juan meets his end. He is called upon to keep his word. He is made to take seriously something at which he had scoffed. He is made the victim of a cruel trick. He is shown that death is not so far away as he had thought and that all deadlines have to be met. In short, Don Juan is made to face the consequences of his actions. This is the idea which is dramatically embodied in the scenes with the statue. The discovery of the Commander's effigy symbolizes the idea that however fast one travels one cannot leave one's past behind. The two invitations symbolize the two sides of a social relationship. Even in small details, Don Juan's punishment may be seen to be appropriate. The invitation "dame esa mano" which he had used against his victims is used against him. Don Juan had offended a foreign King; he is punished by a former ambassador. He repeatedly violated the laws of hospitality; he is punished by a guest turned host. He dishonoured Doña Ana and murdered her father; Don Gonzalo had sworn to be avenged. Don Juan broke up a marriage; he is killed on what was to have been his own wedding night. He played on his victims' sense of honour; he is trapped through his own. He blamed others for what he did to them ("tú la vida te quitaste", II, 537); his own punishment ("el fuego que buscaste", III, 951) is his own fault.

Damnation

The manner of Don Juan's death can be seen to be fitting. Eternal
damnation may still seem to be a harsh sentence. Damnation
in Golden-Age drama is in fact extremely rare. Two fairly well-
known cases are those of Paulo in *El condenado por desconfiado*,
another play generally attributed to Tirso de Molina, and
Nineucio in *Tanto es lo de más como lo de menos*, which is
known to be by him. In neither of these cases is there any room
for doubt. Paulo makes a posthumous appearance surrounded by
flames and serpents and quotes the sentence which was passed on
him. Nineucio is also shown amid the flames of hell, "llamas de
inmortalidad, / castigo de Dios eterno", where "en tormentos
perdurables" he is paying for his sins.[1] Don Juan Tenorio is
threatened with death, judgement and hell; he is given a fore-
taste of hell's torments; he is denied a confessor; there are strong
reasons for thinking that his last-minute repentance is not
genuine; but in neither *B* nor *TL* does the statue mention damnation. What it says is that God wants him to pay for his sins at
the hands of a dead man. Catalinón's account tends to confirm
this. In *B* he reports the statue as saying:

> Dios
> me manda que así te mate,
> castigando tus delitos.
> Quien tal hace, que tal pague. (III, 1047–50)

In *TL* the statue is reported as saying only:

> Dios te castiga,
> "quien tal hace que tal pague". (III, 860–1)

Either version allows of the view that Don Juan's punishment
consists in being killed, and that the flames he feels are those of
purgatory. There is a strong probability that he is damned, but
this time the playwright does not presume to know. The two
things which are certain are that Don Juan is struck dead, "no
shriving-time allowed", and that he dies in great pain.

Theologians and moralists had long preached the dangers of

---

[1] *Obras dramáticas completas*, ed. Blanca de los Ríos (Madrid, 1946), p. 1153a.

last-minute repentance. Fray Luis de Granada, whose *Guía de pecadores* (1556) was still very widely read in the seventeenth century, devotes a whole chapter to the subject (I, xxvi). A number of his quotations and comments can be applied to Don Juan.[2] Of those who wait until they are old before reforming, Fray Luis quotes Seneca as saying that they are only giving to virtue the time which is no good to them for anything else. He also quotes St Gregory as saying that such behaviour is a form of disloyalty:

> Harto lejos está de la fidelidad que debe a Dios, el que espera el tiempo de la vejez para hacer penitencia. Debía este tal temer no venga a caer en las manos de la justicia, esperando indiscretamente en la misericordia. (94b)

The passage he quotes from St Augustine stresses the dangers of death-bed repentance, including the torments of purgatory:

> Y porque hay muchas cosas que en este tiempo impiden el hacer penitencia, peligrosísima cosa es, y muy vecina de la perdición, dilatar hasta la muerte el remedio de ella. Y con todo esto digo que si este tal alcanzare perdón de sus culpas, no por eso quedará libre de todas las penas. Porque primero ha de ser purgado con el fuego del purgatorio por haber dejado el fruto de la satisfacción para el otro siglo. (96a)

On the likelihood that late repentance may not be sincere he quotes Hugh of St Victor:

> Dificultosa cosa es, que sea verdadera la penitencia cuando viene tardía; y muy sospechosa debe ser aquella penitencia que parece forzada. (97a)

The passage which Fray Luis quotes from the Book of Proverbs seems especially applicable to the Burlador:

> Extendí mis manos, y no hubo quien las mirase, y despreciastes todas mis reprehensiones y consejos; yo también me reiré en vuestra muerte, y haré burla de vosotros cuando os vinieren los males que temíades. (98b)

[2] Quotations are from *Obras de Fray Luis de Granada*, I, Biblioteca de Autores Españoles, VI (repr., Madrid, 1944). These are not suggested as sources — merely as illustrations of Golden-Age religious thought. Maurel (*15*) finds similar parallels in the works of Ludovicus Blosius. The need for timely repentance is a common devotional theme.

The emphasis of the play is all on divine justice, not on divine mercy. Its message is much the same as the one with which Luis de Granada ends his chapter "contra los que perseveran en sus pecados con esperanza de la divina misericordia":

> Así, hermano mío, déjate esas presuntuosas confianzas, y acuérdate que hay en Dios misericordia y justicia; por donde así como pones los ojos en la misericordia para esperar, así también los debes poner en la justicia para temer. (105b)

Deception

Deception is one of the most pervasive themes in Spanish literature of the Golden Age, in prose fiction and lyric poetry as well as in drama. Various forms of "burla", from the practical joke to the confidence-trick, form the basis of the picaresque novels. The pastoral novels are full of instances where characters pretend to love one person in order to provoke the jealousy or love of another. Deception and illusion are a central preoccupation of Cervantes, not only in *Don Quijote* but also in the *Novelas ejemplares* and in some of his plays and *entremeses*. Lyric poetry in the second half of the Golden Age is increasingly concerned with the illusory nature of love. All sorts of drama, from *entremeses* and *capa y espada* plays to serious works like *El castigo sin venganza*, *El condenado por desconfiado*, *La vida es sueño* and *La hija del aire* present plots which turn on a deception. Calderón even wrote a play called *En la vida todo es verdad y todo mentira*. There is another one called *No hay que creer ni en la verdad*. Was there ever an age when men and women were so afraid of being deceived? This play about a "burlador" is richly expressive of the general loss of confidence. With Don Juan about, the sexes cannot trust each other ("¡Mal haya la mujer que en hombres fía!", III, 408; "sois los hombres traidores", I, 935; "la mujer más constante / es, en efeto, mujer", I, 357–8. "Al fin, al fin es mujer", III, 68), nor kings their favourites ("¡Esto mis privados hacen!", III, 1028), nor noblemen their friends ("pues como amigo / pudo el cruel engañarme", III, 1018–19). The play uses several of the stock devices of the comedies of intrigue (impersonation in the dark, the exchange of cloaks, an intercepted letter), but these are not used by the characters, as they are in the comedies, in the service of love. Indeed love, like honour and loyalty, is conspicuous by its absence. Social order is restored after Don Juan has been removed, but the foundations have been badly shaken. The play expresses no confidence in humanity's ability to manage its own affairs.

Apart from conventional stage devices and a general disillusionment, deception is an important part of the supernatural ending of this play, for in the end the statue deceives Don Juan.

Don Juan's taunting of the statue, ending in the irreverent invitation to supper, is provoked by the inscription on the tomb:

> Aquí aguarda del Señor
> el más leal caballero
> la venganza de un traidor. (III, 450–2)

The wording is ambiguous. "Here the King's (or the Lord's?) most loyal 'caballero' is awaiting revenge on a traitor (or a traitor's revenge?)." Or "Here the most loyal 'caballero' awaits the Lord's revenge on a traitor". Confronted by this challenge and reproach from the past, Don Juan is not impressed:

> Del mote reírme quiero. (III, 453)

Mockingly, he invites the statue to supper, after which they can fight the duel. When the two are alone together, the statue asks Don Juan to promise to keep his word, then asks him for his hand, in confirmation of the promise. His words are

> Dame esa mano, no temas. (III, 644)

Don Juan rises at once to the challenge. Afterwards he reveals that as soon as the statue took his hand he felt a terrible burning sensation. He soon dismisses his fears as imaginary, but the statue later declares itself to be the agent of divine justice. Is it not disturbing that God's agent should play such a trick? When next they meet he does it again:

> Dame esa mano;
> no temas, la mano dame. (III, 946–7)

This time he does not let go. Is it enough to say that the deceiver deserved – indeed, asked (III, 280) – to be deceived? Are even God's agents not to be trusted?

"Dame esa mano, no temas" : these words sound friendly. If
we compare these scenes with the final scenes of Tirso's *Santa
Juana* trilogy we see that it is just possible that the statue is being
cruel to be kind. At the end of the third *Santa Juana* play a soul
from purgatory appears to the hero, Don Luis. When Don Luis
asks the apparition whether the torments of purgatory are as great
as those of hell the apparition asks for his hand. When he gives
it to him Don Luis, just like Don Juan, feels a burning pain.
This is plainly intended as a warning. A voice speaks to Don
Luis :

> ¡Hombre, que os avisa un alma!
> Mudad el vicioso extremo.[3]

In this case the warning is heeded. Don Luis resolves to change
his way of life. He is reconciled with his father (whom he had
earlier knocked down and kicked) and agrees to marry the girl
to whom he had given his word.[4] As soon as he agrees to keep
his promise the pain in his hand stops. Don Luis had Juana to
intercede for him. Thanks to her he receives this special enlightenment. But it seems possible that if Don Juan had taken
the statue's words as an offer of friendship instead of a provocation he too might have had the chance to repent. The statue does
not grab Don Juan's hand but invites him to give it. Perhaps it is
not too casuistical to see this as a further suggestion that Don Juan
brings the final deception on himself.

Time

Closely linked to the general theme of deception is another
pervasive theme of Golden-Age literature and art : what the poet
Góngora called "la brevedad engañosa de la vida".[5] Human life –
even the life of empires – is fleeting. To forget this, let alone deny

---

[3] Tirso de Molina, *La santa Juana*, ed. Agustín del Campo (Madrid, 1948),
p. 367.

[4] "Pondré la mano en un fuego/que he de cumplir mi palabra" (ed. cit., 368).
The association of an oath with placing one's hand in a fire is a further link
with *El burlador*.

[5] Title of a well-known sonnet (dating from 1623). See Luis de Góngora y
Argote, *Obras completas*, ed J. Millé y Giménez and Isabel Millé y Giménez (Madrid,
1956), pp. 525-6.

it, is to be deceived. Whenever death or judgement are mentioned Don Juan's retort is always that there is plenty of time ("¡Qué largo me lo fiáis!", I, 904; "De aquí allá hay gran jornada", II, 406). Death, when one is young and vigorous, seems a long way away. But it may not be ("Breve te ha de parecer", II, 407). In any case the day of reckoning cannot be indefinitely put off ("No hay plazo que no llegue", III, 932). All debts must be settled in the end. Don Juan refuses to face this – jauntily at first, later on by lashing out. Although he is always in such a hurry, he is, morally, a procrastinator. He deceives himself in thinking he has plenty of time.

Don Juan is young and youth is impetuous. His impatience is in character. It ensures that the play does not drag. It also gives the play a moral urgency, by showing a hero who is rushing to destruction. The play's sense of breathless urgency, of time running out and of inexorable retribution, is in some ways the dramatic equivalent of the sonnet, written by a contemporary of Tirso, Pedro Soto de Rojas (1584–1658):

Aviso
¿Dónde, di, caminante, vas perdido,
tras la posta veloz de tu pecado,
del apetito tu ofensor cargado,
calzado muerte, corrupción vestido?

¿Dónde, arroyuelo, corres tan crecido?
¿Dónde vas, torbellino, tan hinchado?
Al centro amargo vas precipitado:
a deshacerte al fin constituído.

Detén, reprime el paso, vuelve, y mira
lo que te espera al fin de la jornada;
pues caminas sin luz, teme, suspira.

Teme, pues eres carne, ardiente espada;
teme, pues tú lo incitas, justa ira;
teme, pues rompes ley, sentencia dada.[6]

Ultimately the dramatic force of this play (like that of Marlowe's *Dr Faustus*) depends on the drama inherent in the Christian

---

[6] *An Anthology of Spanish Poetry, 1500-1700*, ed. Arthur Terry, Part II (Oxford, 1968), p. 151.

view of life and of the last things (Death, Judgement, Heaven and Hell). The ending of the story of any Christian soul is not decided until the last minute. And one never knows when the last minute may come. Actions performed in the temporal world may be decisive for all eternity. The two Spanish plays which most successfully exploit this peculiarly Christian dramatic potential are *El condenado por desconfiado* and *El burlador*.

Credit (Trust)

"¡Qué largo me lo fiáis!" : Don Juan's motto brings together the ideas of time, trust and payment, or, in a word, credit. Like other confidence-tricksters, Don Juan is out to get something for nothing. He offers to marry his victims as the price of getting into bed with them and he has no intention of paying. When it is pointed out to him that he will have to pay in the end he replies that there is plenty of time. Don Juan is living on moral credit. He can be called a confidence-trickster rather than merely a reckless overspender because he deliberately creates trust in order to betray it. He produces false promises of marriage like a false credit-card. His first words are the renewal of a false promise to Isabela, roughly the equivalent of forging Octavio's signature on a cheque. To Tisbea he offers his hand and his word ("Esta es mi mano y mi fe"). His trick with Ana's letter is an attempt at misappropriation: he is entrusted with the letter on the strength of being a gentleman and Mota's friend. With Aminta and Gaseno, he obtains credit through impressing them with his fine clothes and powerful connections. All his *burlas* are variants on the *perro muerto*, a form of cheating whores of their fee. In one important respect they differ from the ploys of other confidence-tricksters: far from trying to evade detection, Don Juan, in order to humiliate his victims and their protectors, needs to be found out. Not satisfied with betraying trust, Don Juan derides it. His abuse of moral credit brings the whole system into disrepute. The swindler must be made to pay so that confidence may be restored.

But the exposure of swindlers can destroy confidence as well as restoring it. *Desengaño* is not at all the same as simple faith.

Honour

The question of credit, or trust, brings us back to the central paradox in Don Juan's behaviour: he prides himself on being a "burlador"; he also prides himself on being a man of his word ("Honor / tengo y las palabras cumplo / porque caballero soy", III, 641–3). All his "burlas" depend on broken promises, yet he dies rather than break his word. One way of resolving this paradox might be to say that the promises he breaks are made to women, whereas the one he insists on keeping is made to a fellow-"caballero". But then Don Juan also breaks his word to his uncle and lies to his friend Mota. A more plausible explanation is that his decision to keep his word to the statue shows the beginning of a new seriousness (*14*). But perhaps the paradox can best be resolved by considering his conduct in terms of honour. When he breaks his promises to the women he dishonours them (and also their male protectors). If he failed to keep his promise to the statue he would bring dishonour to himself. He keeps his promise – and gives his hand – when not to do so would look like cowardice. This explanation may be a little too pat. Much of the power of Don Juan's last scenes derives from their air of mystery, from the fact that we are not told what is going on in the hero's mind. But it is clear that Don Juan sets great value on his reputation for courage and reacts sharply to any suggestion that he may be afraid (*2*).

In the light of this, the Commander's epitaph and the statue's invitation may be seen as a well-laid trap. The epitaph refers to revenge on a traitor, but in his dying words Don Gonzalo had linked treachery with cowardice:

> el que es traidor
> es traidor porque es cobarde. (II, 543–4)

When the statue asks Don Juan for his hand, it tells him not to be afraid (III, 644). Don Juan rises promptly to the bait:

> ¿Eso dices? ¿Yo temor?
> Si fueras el mismo infierno
> la mano te diera yo. (III, 645–7)

He says later that if he does not keep his appointment the dead man will denounce him as "infame" (III, 871–2). When the statue expresses mild surprise that Don Juan should have kept his word, Don Juan asks hotly:

> ¿Me tienes
> en opinión de cobarde? (III, 891–2)

He rises manfully to each subsequent test of his courage. When told he must lift up the tombstone he offers to uproot the pillars as well. The statue encourages his recklessness with a well-judged compliment: "valiente estás" (III, 906). Don Juan's retort is boastful (and, to a stone statue, perhaps also tactless): "Tengo brío y corazón en las carnes" (III, 906–7). He will eat whatever the statue cares to put in front of him. Even after the warning words of the song he rises to the statue's provocation exactly as he did the first time:

DON GONZALO: Dame esa mano;
                       no temas, la mano dame.

DON JUAN: ¿Eso dices? ¿Yo temor? (III, 946–8)

And the trap shuts. What Don Juan says of Batricio the statue could say of Don Juan: "con el honor le vencí" (III, 101).

Does the supposed "caballerosidad" of Don Juan consist of anything more than this: pride in his own courage? He saves his servant from drowning when he himself is on the point of exhaustion. In this servant's eyes he is (except where women are concerned) a perfect gentleman:

> Como no le entreguéis vos
> moza o cosa que lo valga,
> bien podéis fiaros dél;
> que en cuanto en esto es cruel,
> tiene condición hidalga. (II, 161–5)

But we have already seen that his uncle was wrong to trust him. Quite apart from that, to be chivalrous except where young women are concerned is not to be chivalrous at all. Not only in his treatment of the fair sex, but in his behaviour towards everybody else – his disrespect for the crown, his disobedience to his

father and his uncle, his ingratitude for hospitality, his betrayal
of friends, his irreverence for a fallen enemy – and in his un-
concern about the fate of his immortal soul, he is, as A. A. Parker
has said (27), "the negation of 'caballerosidad' ".[7] His sense of
honour is not worthy of respect because he has no respect for
other people's.

Courage

There is still no denying his courage. Unlike Don Gonzalo (and,
incidentally, unlike Lope's villainous "comendadores"), he has
no record of war service. His reputation as the "Hector of
Seville" has been earned not by gallantry in the field but by outrageous "mocedades". But these are undoubtedly dangerous. He
defies the Neapolitan palace guard (while at the same time
insisting on diplomatic immunity). He is prepared (probably not
for the first time) to climb down from a high balcony. He saves
his servant from drowning. He refuses to be daunted by the
statue come to life.

Is his courage held up for unqualified admiration? On this
question the views on different types of bravery put forward by
the fourteenth-century moralist Don Juan Manuel may shed a
little indirect light. With characteristic thoroughness the Infante
divides men into four classes: the "omne esforçado", the
"quexoso", the "medroso" and the "spantoso". None of these
terms is easy to translate, but Juan Manuel defines them as follows: the "esforçado" is "el que ha efuerço quando lo deve aver,
et en las cosas que lo deve aver". The "quexoso" on the other
hand "es el que á esfuerço quando lo deve aver et ha esfuerço
quando non lo deve aver, ca la quexa del coraçón non le dexa
sofrir el miedo". The "medroso" "á efuerço quando lo deve aver,
et miedo quando lo deve aver". The "espantoso" is afraid of
everything – "ha miedo et spántase de lo que deve aver miedo et

---

[7] The disagreement between Parker and J. Pitt-Rivers ("Honour and Social
Status", in *Honour and Shame: the values of Mediterranean society*, ed. J. G.
Peristiany [London, 1965], p. 33) on this point is more apparent than real. Pitt-
Rivers argues that, according to one view of honour still current in Latin coun-
tries, Don Juan is a "man of honour"; but he concedes that "the theme of the
play is, precisely, a critique of this theory of honour – a fact which is surely
congruent with the fact that the author was a priest" (p. 77 n. 23).

72						El burlador de Sevilla

espántase de lo que non ha razón por que deve aver miedo". Don
Juan Tenorio appears to belong to the second of these four
classes. What Juan Manuel goes on to say about the "quexoso"
seems to describe his case exactly: "el quexoso da a entender
que non ha miedo de ninguna cosa, et non cata en ello razón nin
cordura, et así como lo comiença sin razón, así saldrá ende mucho
aýna sin razón".[8] Juan Manuel was writing his Libro del caballero for the guidance of young men of just Don Juan Tenorio's
social class, and also, as it happens, in the reign of Alfonso XI
of Castile. The young Tenorio's much-vaunted courage would
not have greatly impressed him. There is no need to suppose that
the playwright knew the Libro del caballero. It may still be worth
remembering that a true-blue Spanish nobleman could distinguish
between courage and foolhardiness. It is also perhaps worth
noting that another famous comedia probably written at very
much the same time as El burlador refers specifically to something called "necio valor". This is Lope de Vega's El caballero
de Olmedo.[9] Interestingly enough, the climax of this play too
presents a hero who goes to his death rather than be seen to give
in to fear.[10] J. W. Sage has shown that at the time when El
caballero was written the "caballero" was a figure who had come
to be regarded with less respect and affection than heretofore.[11]
Aminta's remark that "La desvergüenza en España / se ha hecho
caballería" (III, 131–2) may reflect a general attitude.

As we have seen, El burlador shows the aristocracy (and nearly
everybody else) in an unflattering light. Like a number of
thoughtful plays of the period it can be seen as attacking
contemporary debasements of the once noble values of honour
and courage.

[8] Juan Manuel, Libro del cavallero et del escudero, in Obras de Don Juan
Manuel, ed. J. M. Castro y Calvo and M. de Riquer, I (Barcelona, 1955), p. 32.
[9] Ed. I. I. Macdonald (Cambridge, repr. 1971), p. 94, line 2409.
[10] Although the two heroes are so different in other respects, the parallel here
is close. Don Alonso refuses to turn back because "En mi nobleza / fuera ese
temor bajeza". He dismisses the warnings as imaginary and asks " ¿qué han de
decir si me vuelvo?" (pp. 94-5, lines 2407-23).
[11] J. W. Sage, Lope de Vega: "El caballero de Olmedo" (Critical Guides to
Spanish Texts, 6, London, 1974), pp. 24-34.

In literary criticism all conclusions are provisional, but a Critical Guide still has to try to reach them. *El Burlador de Sevilla* is not, and possibly never was, a polished or a delicate work of art. Its strengths are those of its two protagonists – on the one hand daring and vitality, on the other, imposing authority – plus the force of the confrontation between them. There is ingenuity displayed in the web of mutual deceptions. What I have called the play's "fearful symmetry" (*10*) offers some rather grim aesthetic and moral satisfaction. Emotionally the whole work is rather crude. There is no tenderness or delicacy of feeling. Nor is there, for all the wit and excitement, much joy. The country wedding-song and Tisbea's first speech show some delight in the beauties of nature, but the pleasure is short-lived. The beauty of woman is a temptation to man and a danger to herself. Passions are not to be trusted. The harsh laughter of Don Juan is countered by the harsh pronouncements of the statue.

Tough-minded and authoritarian, this is very much a man's play, even a celibate's play. It has been most aptly described as a "Lenten sermon" (*6*). Bleakly pessimistic about human society and human nature, it is not quite despairing – for to try to frighten human beings into behaving better implies a hope, however faint, that they are capable of improvement (there is also, in the description of Lisbon, a glimpse of society as it should be). The fierce punishment meted out to the vices of deceitfulness, malice, flippancy and presumption implies a belief in at least the possibility of trustworthiness, goodwill, respect and humility. The playwright's skill in playing on the emotions of his audience is very much a preacher's (*15, 23*). So is his urgent concern for their moral welfare. If his treatment of his hero is harsh, this is so that his audience may profit from the example. Like many a pulpit-thumping priest, he is (perhaps not without a certain relish) being cruel to be kind.

Has this forthright dramatic sermon anything to say to a

I cannot
it does !!

foreign, twentieth-century audience who may not share the preacher's beliefs? I have suggested that a large part of the play's force derives from a Christian view of death and the here-after. An audience who do not believe in hell fire may well find the death of Don Juan less awe-inspiring. But the decline in belief in damnation has not removed the fear of death; nor has the idea of justice enshrined in the words "Quien tal hace que tal pague" lost its force. In all sorts of spheres – personal, professional, commercial, industrial, political, diplomatic – trust is still both necessary and vulnerable. Perhaps the conflict between Don Juan and the statue can be related to something as deep-seated in human nature as the conflict between id and superego (two entities just as mythical and not half as memorable as the play's protagonists). In an age when prophecies of doom are more often concerned with ecology than with eschatology the opposition between "¡Qué largo me lo fiáis!" and "Quien tal hace que tal pague" has taken on new meaning without losing any of its power to disturb. Irresponsibility is still exciting, dangerous and wrong. "Quien tal hace que tal pague" still makes sense.

Bibliographical Note

1. Joaquín Casalduero, *Contribución al estudio del tema de don Juan en el teatro español*, Smith College Studies in Modern Languages, XIX, nos. 3/4 (Northampton, Mass, 1938). Reprinted with a new introduction (Madrid, 1975). Modern critical appreciation of *El burlador* begins here. C exaggerates the differences between *B* and *TL*. Since he dates *B* before *TL* his explanations of the differences must also be misleading. Nevertheless C first perceived the organic unity and underlying themes of *B*.

2. E. H. Templin, "The *burla* in the Plays of Tirso de Molina", *Hispanic Review*, VIII (1940), 185–201. Examines the various senses covered by the word as used by Tirso. Some perceptive comments on Don Juan, but the arrangement is scrappy and the language abstruse.

3. I. L. McClelland, *Tirso de Molina. Studies in dramatic realism* (Liverpool, 1948). See especially ch. II and ch. VII. Recaptures the excitement of the supernatural scenes and speculates interestingly on Don Juan's state of mind. The idea that the moving statue is a figment of Don Juan's imagination is not borne out by the text.

4. G. Delpy, "Réflexions sur *El burlador de Sevilla*", *Bulletin Hispanique*, L (1948), 463–71. Some perceptive comment but no definite conclusion.

5. Archimede Marni, "Did Tirso Employ Counter-Passion in his *Burlador de Sevilla?*", *Hispanic Review*, XX (1952), 123–33. Suggests that, like Dante, Tirso may have applied this Aristotelian-Thomist concept in making punishment fit crime. M's conclusion that the statue's words "imply no deceit" runs counter to his own evidence and argument, which point rather to the conclusion that the deceiver deserves to be deceived.

6. Charles V. Aubrun, "Le Don Juan de Tirso de Molina: essai d'interprétation", *Bulletin Hispanique*, LIX (1957), 26-61. A brilliant essay. Clears away Romantic misconceptions and stresses the disillusioned picture of society. Exaggerates the play's incoherence, takes liberties with the text and underrates the importance of the double invitation.

7. Bruce W. Wardropper, "*El burlador de Sevilla*: a tragedy of errors", *Philological Quarterly*, XXXVI (1957), 61-71. Brings out the fallibility of all the major characters with the exception of Ana [?] and her father. Like 6, emphasizes *desengaño*.

8. Leo Weinstein, *The Metamorphoses of Don Juan* (Stanford, 1959). Contains a very good chapter on *El burlador*. Sees the play's intrinsic merits as well as its historical importance.

9. Heinrich Bihler, "Más detalles sobre ironía, simetría y simbolismo en *El burlador de Sevilla* de Tirso de Molina", in *Actas del primer congreso internacional de hispanistas* (Oxford, 1964), pp. 213–18. Good on irony and symmetry. The suggestions on the symbolism of vowel-sounds may seem farfetched, but the repetitions are there in the text.

10. Daniel Rogers, " 'Fearful Symmetry': the ending of *El burlador de Sevilla*", *Bulletin of Hispanic Studies*, XLI (1964), 141-59. Points to links between the ending and the rest and argues that these are more effective in *B* than in *TL*.

76 *El burlador de Sevilla*

11. C. B. Morris, "Metaphor in *El burlador de Sevilla*", *Romanic Review*, LV (1964), 248-55. Argues subtly and, on the whole, persuasively for the play's "poetic coherence".

12. Gerald E. Wade, "The Character of Don Juan of *El burlador de Sevilla*", in *Hispanic Studies in Honor of Nicholson B. Adams*, ed. J. E. Keller and K.-L. Selig, University of North Carolina Studies in the Romance Languages and Literatures, LIX (Chapel Hill, North Carolina, 1966), pp. 167–78. A very sensible description based on "the facts of the play". Summarized in Introduction to *34*.

13. Mathé Allain, " 'El burlador burlado': Tirso de Molina's Don Juan", *Modern Language Quarterly*, XXVII (1966), 174-84. An elegant and ingenious account of the mutual deceptions. Only the argument for the relevance of the Lisbon speech seems strained.

14. Ion Tudor Agheana and Henry Sullivan, "The Unholy Martyr: Don Juan's misuse of intelligence ", *Romanische Forschungen*, LXXXI (1969), 311–25. Full of bright ideas, notably that Don Juan is an adroit manipulator" until outwitted by the statue. That Don Juan dies in a state of enlightenment is not verifiable in the text.

15. Serge Maurel, *L'Univers dramatique de Tirso de Molina* (Poitiers, 1971). A masterly chapter on *El burlador* forms the climax of this important book.

16. Ion Tudor Agheana, *The Situational Drama of Tirso de Molina* (Madrid, 1972). Points out how often Tirso's plays have one character who manipulates the action. (Suggests the possible influence of *La Celestina*.) A good short account of this aspect of Don Juan.

17. Charles V. Aubrun, "L'Imposteur floué et le repas en enfer, comédie méconnue de Tirso", *Hispanic Review*, XLI (1973), 161-9. A further ingenious attempt to demythologize Don Juan. Full of brilliant suggestions, but some are far-fetched. One such, based on a simple textual error, is corrected by Xavier A. Fernández in *Romance Notes*, XV (1973-4), 564-5.

18. Robert ter Horst, "The *loa* of Lisbon and the Mythical Substructure of *El burlador de Sevilla*", *Bulletin of Hispanic Studies*, L (1973), 147-65. A persuasive and elegant defence of the relevance of the Lisbon speech. Some of the connections are surprising but they all repay consideration.

19. Bruce W. Wardropper, "El tema central de *El burlador de Sevilla*", *Segismundo*, XVII-XVIII (1973), 9-16. W takes this to be the fallibility of human justice and the need for divine intervention.

20. Arturo Serrano Plaja, "Un no de Don Juan y un no a Don Juan", *Segismundo*, XVII-XVIII (1973), 17-31. Some valuable further suggestions on the play's coherence.

21. Robert ter Horst, "On the Character of Don Juan in *El burlador de Sevilla*", *Segismundo*, XVII-XVIII (1973), 33–42. Interprets "character" as "theological identity" rather than the "peculiarities of a given psycho-sexual constitution". Less convincing than *18*. Describes the play a seventeenth-century dramatist might have written.

22. Carlos Feal Deibe, "El *burlador* de Tirso y la mujer", *Symposium*, XXIX (1975), 300-13. An excellent study of the imagery relating to women and to sexual love. Brings out the playwright's "concepción frailuna y misógina de la vida".

Four more general works are well worth consulting on *El burlador*:

23. Charles V. Aubrun, *La Comédie espagnole (1600-1800)* (Paris, 1966), pp. 67-9. Acknowledges the play's studied construction (cf. 6). Good on the playwright's skill as a preacher.
24. Margaret Wilson, *Spanish Drama of the Golden Age* (Oxford, 1968). Contains (pp. 124-9) an excellent concise account of *El burlador*. The whole book is strongly recommended.
25. Edward M. Wilson and Duncan Moir, *The Golden Age: Drama 1492-1700*, in *A Literary History of Spain*, ed. R. O. Jones (London and New York, 1971), pp. 88-91. Packed with intelligent and provocative comment.
26. P. E. Russell, in *Spain: a companion to Spanish studies*, ed. Russell (London, 1973), pp. 362-3. Much less enthusiastic. A good corrective to some of the others.

Two important essays on Golden-Age drama contain some valuable observations on *El burlador*:

27. A. A. Parker, *The Approach to the Spanish Drama of the Golden Age*, Diamante, VI (London, 1957). Helpful both because of its specific references and because *El burlador* is a play which responds particularly well to P's approach.
28. Bruce W. Wardropper, "The Implicit Craft of the Spanish *comedia*", in *Studies in Spanish Literature of the Golden Age presented to Edward M. Wilson*, ed. R. O. Jones (London, 1973), pp. 339-56. Chooses *El burlador* as an example of a play which is "triumphantly coherent by poetic standards".

Textual Studies

29. Gerald E. Wade and Robert J. Mayberry, "*Tan largo me lo fiais* and *El burlador de Sevilla y el* [sic] *convidado de piedra*", *Bulletin of the Comediantes*, XIV, 1 (1962), 1-16.
30. María Rosa Lida de Malkiel, "Sobre la prioridad de ¿*Tan largo me lo fiáis?* Notas al *Isidro* y a *El burlador de Sevilla*", *Hispanic Review*, XXX (1962), 275-95.
31. Albert E. Sloman, "The Two Versions of *El burlador de Sevilla*", *Bulletin of Hispanic Studies*, XLII (1965), 18-33.

All three articles argue for the priority of *TL*. The editor of 32 takes the opposite view.

Editions

32. *Tan largo me lo fiáis*, ed. Xavier A. Fernández (Madrid, 1967).
33. *El burlador de Sevilla*, ed. Américo Castro (Madrid, 1910). Revised and several times reprinted (with *El vergonzoso en palacio*) in Clásicos Castellanos series. Still the best edition for sixth forms and universities.
34. *El burlador de Sevilla y convidado de piedra*, ed. Gerald E. Wade (New York, 1969). Full of historical information. W's theory concerning Claramonte's part in *B* is not proven.
35. Arcadio Baquero, *Don Juan y su evolución dramática*, 2 vols (Madrid, 1966). Brings together texts of *TL*, *B* and four later Don Juan plays. The introduction to each text is superficial.